LIFE SENTENCE PRISONERS

LIFE SENTENCE PRISONERS

Reaction, Response and Change

R. J. Sapsford

Open University Press

Milton Keynes

Open University Press
A division of
Open University Educational Enterprises Limited
12 Cofferidge Close
Stony Stratford
Milton Keynes MK11 1BY, England.

First published 1983
Copyright © 1983 Roger Sapsford

British Library Cataloguing in Publication Data

Sapsford, R. J.
  Life sentence prisoners
  1. Life imprisonment – Great Britain
  I. Title
  365'.6   HV8711

ISBN 0-335-10413-4

Text design by W.A.P.

Typeset by Oxford Verbatim Limited
Printed in Great Britain by
The Thetford Press Limited, Thetford, Norfolk

CONTENTS

Contents

List of Tables

List of Figures

ACKNOWLEDGEMENTS

I take full responsibility for all mistakes, oversimplifications and failures of empathy in what follows, but I must acknowledge a great debt to a large number of people without whom this book could not be as it is. My sincere thanks go to Charlotte Banks and Rodney Maliphant, who started some of the ideas, to Brian Emes, Alistair Papps, David Smith and Steven Folkard for smoothing the way and to the prisoners and prison staff who found time and patience to talk to me. Parts of the last chapter were discussed extensively with Pamela Abbott and Wendy Stainton Rogers, to the point where I cannot clearly distinguish my ideas from theirs. (It was Pamela who encouraged me to persevere with this book.) Debbie Coast typed the manuscript (several times, I'm afraid), for which sincere thanks are due. Finally my grateful thanks are due to Alaisdair, Francesca and the D307 Course Team, without whom it would all have been ready earlier.

Please note that in the making of any general points in this book, 'he' stands for 'he or she'. In this instance, the convention seems appropriate, as all the lifers who are the subjects of my research are men.

1

INTRODUCTION –

a project on life sentence prisoners

This book originates in a study of sixty life sentence prisoners I undertook in 1975 when I was employed as part of the 'prisons team' of the Home Office Research Unit (HORU) under the general direction of Dr Charlotte Banks. The 'factual' material in it has mostly appeared elsewhere in more detailed but less accessible form (Sapsford, 1978, 1979a, 1979b). My purpose here is not just to convey the results of a piece of criminological research, however, but to suggest what the psychology of 'life' in prison can tell us about the nature of life outside and also to reflect on the nature of the research process itself.

There are thus four 'stories' of the research which the book has to tell:

1. The research may be seen as part of an institutional research programme mounted by the Home Office, and as such shaped by the concerns of Prison Department at the time when the fieldwork was undertaken.
2. At the same time it was a piece of academic work undertaken for a doctoral thesis, partly supervised from University College London, which applied an essentially laboratory-based model of reactions to stress and deprivation to a real prison population.
3. The book also documents the successive 'readings' of the data at which I have arrived as my psychological concerns have shifted gradually from a quantitative and 'scientific' psychology of human reaction to a more qualitative and interpretative concern with how people respond to crises and how they cope with life (and sometimes even change it) by the process of construing it.
4. Finally, the process of reinterpretation has led me to

speculate on the nature of social psychology itself, as a human activity which itself stands in need of some analysis and interpretation.

(The elements are listed here in the order of their importance at the time when the research was conducted, but in the project's 'afterlife' the order has become reversed. If this book is about any one 'thing', then its subject is the nature of 'doing psychology' as an activity.)

'Institutionalization' was the topic I took up for my thesis research – reported in Chapter 3 and more fully in Sapsford (1979a) – and a project was designed to test a hypothesis derived from Seligman's theories of 'learned helplessness' (Seligman, 1975). Prisons, mental hospitals and concentration camps have four things in common: their inmates suffer a complete break in lifestyle; they are generally interned against their will; the sentence is of indeterminate duration (certainly for lifers, and to some extent for other prisoners because of parole); and even trivial aspects of life – having a bath, going to the toilet – are controllable by the authorities. The net result is an environment over which the inmate has virtually no control; he is subject to vast numbers of rules and restrictions which are not of his own making. When you subject animals to an unpleasant experience and condition them to the knowledge that nothing they can do will have any effect on it, a proportion of them show initial anxiety and distress but soon lapse into almost total apathy; faced later with an aversive stimulus which is in fact escapable, they make no effort to escape. Similar results have been obtained with human subjects, and here subjects tend to report that 'Nothing I can do makes any difference, so there's no point in my trying – I might as well give up.' Seligman has pointed out strong similarities between this laboratory phenomenon and the clinical phenomenon of reactive depression. Now, prison would seem to be an excellent example of an aversive stimulus which is not contingent on the behaviour of the subject, so we might expect it to provoke learned helplessness: initial anxiety and frenzied activity tailing off into apathy, routinization, dependence and depression (i.e., institutionalization).

Two other pieces of research on long-term imprisonment which reached the report stage in the early 1970s, when my own work was being planned, have influenced me greatly. Of these one was a Home Office sponsored project conducted by four researchers from Durham University, F. V. Smith, Peter Banister, Neil Bolton and K. J. Heskin, who published eight papers on the results between 1973 and 1977. The other was *Psychological Survival* by Stan Cohen and Laurie Taylor.

The Durham University project constituted an elegant demonstration that intellectual ability as measured by formal tests does not decline as a function of imprisonment. A cross-sectional survey of six hundred long-term prisoners, grouped for analysis according to the total time they had spent in prison on this or any previous sentence, failed to show any significant pattern of deterioration on a wide range of intelligence and performance tests; there was some deterioration on complex problem solving but overall the scores did not covary with time served, and indeed there was some improvement in verbal intelligence over time. A longitudinal comparison of scores a year or so later showed the same pattern of results, and similar results were also obtained in a 'comparison group' of people outside measured over the same period. An extensive selection of trait and personality tests was also applied, plus semantic differential scales to measure attitudes to self and significant others inside and outside prison.

In the reports of this research, as in most psychological work in prisons, it would be possible to forget that the subjects of the research were real people serving real prison sentences. The subjects described by Cohen and Taylor, on the other hand, could not be anything other than prisoners: the first and most lasting impression the book makes is that prison is a real, painful and degrading place. One of the book's greatest merits is the immediacy with which it conveys prisoners' fears that prison destroys the mind. Take, for example, this passage reproduced from pages 114–15:

> When Roy arrived to start his twenty-five year sentence some screws tried to reassure him. 'Look at Dawson', they said, pointing to the top landing, 'he's been in for nearly twenty years and he's perfectly content'. Roy would not accept this consolation: 'How could I know if he was content? Anyway what was he content *about*?' Roy's fear was that he might lapse into a state of contentment which marked a departure from reality, but which he did not recognise as such.
>
> The long term prisoners all felt like this. Over the years they have asked us to comment on any signs of deterioration we observed, to record their personality changes, to discuss their cultural inadequacies and their social maladjustments. Not that

we are really needed to point out any signs of deterioration. The men we have met are only too ready to do it for each other. One evening they all sat discussing the future programme for the class. The regular group was trying to decide for the best dates for a new set of lectures. 'Well, Stan's here on Friday' said Paul. 'Monday' said Roy, 'Today's Friday, *you're going*.' 'I'm not – anybody could make that mistake. My mother gets the days mixed. There's nothing special about that.'

The incident is trivial but it indicates the obsessive concern with signs of deterioration and the self-consciousness with which such fears were faced. These men felt that all around them were examples of people who had turned into cabbages because they had not been sufficiently vigilant. Every day they encountered an old sex offender who spent hours merely cleaning and filling the teapot, a mindless activity which the old man appeared to be contented with. And this was their problem: at what price would they achieve peace of mind and contentment? Would they start behaving like the old man, as a way of banishing the ghosts of time, the fear of deterioration and not knowing what was happening to them? In other words, would the cumulative result of years of working at something which looked like adaptation, in fact really be a process of learning how to deteriorate?

The powerful statements which this book makes about how prisoners assess their own lives in prison and what strategies they adopt for dealing with the deprivations of time and career, the loss of personal control and the fear of mental decay have had a great influence on all prison research since its publication in 1972.

What Cohen and Taylor do *not* demonstrate, however, is that deterioration does actually occur as a result of long-term imprisonment. That something is feared does not prove that it occurs, and the presence of apparently institutionalized men in prison does not show that prison leads to institutionalization. The Durham University study shows that 'intelligence' – intellectual potential as assessed by formal tests – does not appear to decline as a function of imprisonment, but that it should decline was in any case an unlikely outcome. More likely, looking at descriptions in institutionalization such as the one from the Advisory Council report (1968), is a decline in the capacity to take decisions, to live with uncertainties and in general to cope with the open world outside, and these would not appear to be measured by a test of cognitive ability; they pertain more to the framework of attitudes, beliefs and general 'set' out of which such abilities are used. The Smith work included measurement of generalized personality traits and of attitudes to various key figures, but few of their measures bear directly on the kinds of change discussed above. (Both studies also confound together life-sentence prisoners with men serving determinate sentences.) Thus there was scope for a further study to extend Smith's results, patterned after his research, but with a larger element of informal, 'ethnographic' or 'biographical' data-collection – to enable variables to emerge in the analysis which the researcher had not previously envisaged, to find out what prisoners do and think as well as how they 'react' to environmental pressure, and in general to reflect some of the strengths of the Cohen and Taylor work.

The more qualitative or appreciative aspect of the work was originally included primarily as expansion and 'local colour' for the more formal and quantitative side. Anticipating Chapter 3, however, the quantitative side of the work failed altogether to show measurable deterioration which could be attributed to prison as a causal agency; instead, the men found ways of coping and preserving some level of autonomy. The interview material and the less neatly measurable aspects of behaviour and attitude recorded in the prison files came therefore to assume a great deal more importance. In part the shift of emphasis was in a sense 'forced on me by the data'; if I wanted to write about anything, it had to be about the strategies and tactics of how people coped. In part, however, the change in emphasis was also a response to a change in paradigm within my own way of viewing psychology and the task of the psychologist. In the long process of fieldwork – which entailed spending more than a fortnight a month for over a year talking to prisoners and prison staff, reading prison files and eating in a prison staff training college – the feelings of the *immediacy* of the research task which reading Cohen and Taylor had stirred up were very strongly reinforced. I rapidly lost interest in the causes of behaviour and in failures of coping; I became interested instead in the fact that men did *not* fail to cope and in how to characterize men's reactions to and decisions about this fundamentally strange and alien environment. Then in the project's afterlife of interpretation, subsequent to the fieldwork, I came to realize that what the men did about their imprisonment was *not* fundamentally strange or alien but could be paralleled in my own life and in those of friends and acquaintances around me in the outside world. In other words, the focus of interest in the study began to move, for me, from coping with prison conditions to how we all cope in our everyday lives and what we understand of them. Although the research which this book describes was carried out in a prison, therefore, it is not a book about prison life, but about all life. Prison has been conceptualized as just one strange and extreme environment which allows the patterns of normal life to be seen more clearly by the very fact that the 'frame' is so alien to our normal expectations.

Finally, Chapter 5 stands back a step to consider the nature of psychology as a research activity, completing the 'intellectual autobiography' which the book represents. From Chapter 4 it should be evident that the psychology of the whole and inter-preting person in action, with no particular emphasis placed on the causal antecedents of behaviour, cannot be a science in the positivistic sense which has been implicit in much psychology until comparatively recently, and it seems appropriate to ask just what kind of an animal it in fact is. Chapter 5 attempts to locate the work which is described earlier in the book among the new-formed traditions of what might loosely be called the 'new psychologies' and to examine what use such endeavours may be. I have suggested that psychology is (and indeed always has been) a political and applied activity akin to therapy or to political philosophy but taking a more individualistic perspec-tive and aiming to provide the material out of which new and more fulfilling personal worlds may be created. Parallels are drawn with the 'critical theory' of Habermas and Marcuse and the 'critical criminology' or 'new criminology' of Taylor, Walton and Young, and an argument is made for the relevance and necessity of a 'critical social psychology' along similar lines but concerned with distinctively psychological issues.

In the course of all these 'steps backward' from the original fieldwork, inevitably, we may travel some way from the immediate experience of life imprisonment, in the direction of what may seem to be complacent abstractions and generaliza-tions. It is difficult to convey what the sentence is like for the people who serve it, in a book most of whose purpose is to discuss theoretical and 'academic' models. I have made some attempt to convey the 'flavour' of the sentence, but the researcher inevitably carried his own 'machinery' of attitudes and sensibilities into the fieldwork. Judging by what was said to me in interviews, the account which I have given grossly understates the problems for some prisoners but equally grossly overstates them for others. The process of abstraction to find common patterns evens out these differences into an 'average' or 'type' which may not be typical of the experience of any individual prisoner, and this problem should be kept in mind while reading what follows.

Finally, while I shall argue that the problems of prisoners differ from those of people outside in degree rather than in kind, this is not to say that prison is in any sense a pleasant or a normal place. On the contrary, few who have not seen the inside of prison can comprehend the degree to which the environment and its rules and deprivations constrict the inmate and bear down on him, and I doubt if anyone except the lifers themselves will ever understand what it is like to serve a sentence with no release date fixed and with no known or certain criteria for release.

2

THE LIFE SENTENCE
IN BRITAIN

This chapter sets the context of the research which is discussed in the remainder of the book. The first section describes the size and composition of the life-sentence population at the time when the research was carried out and its phenomenal rate of growth since the mid-1950s. The nature of the regime to which lifers are exposed in prison is discussed from two points of view; the published intentions of Prison Department are contrasted with what the day-to-day reality may be like for the individuals concerned. Finally, what research there has been on the effects of this regime is briefly outlined.

2.1: *The lifer population*

Most of the population of life-sentence prisoners in England and Wales were convicted of the crime of murder, for which the life sentence has been the sole and mandatory penalty since the Murder (Abolition of Death Penalty) Act 1965, and the only alternative to the death penalty before that date. It is also available and used, however, as the maximum penalty for a range of other offences – homicides other than murder (of which the largest category is 'manslaughter by reason of diminished responsibility'), attempted murder, grievous bodily harm with intent, rape (including unlawful sexual intercourse with a girl younger than thirteen), buggery, robbery, arson and offences under the various 'Explosives Acts'. In 1975, when my field-work commenced, the male lifer population stood at well over a thousand, of whom about 80 per cent had been convicted of murder, about 8 per cent of diminished-responsibility man-slaughter and about 12 per cent of other offences.

Lifers form only a small proportion of the total sentenced prison population – about 3 per cent in 1975, if we include young people sentenced to indefinite detention 'until Her Majesty's Pleasure be known' among the lifers and borstal lads among the prison population. They came to be seen as a 'management problem' by Prison Department – and therefore to attract research effort – not because they bulk large in the prison population but because their numbers increased at an alarming rate in the sixties and seventies, to the point where it was felt that individual initiatives had to be replaced by some kind of systematic policy.

From the mid 1950s to the late 1970s, annual receptions of

FIGURE 1: Male life sentence receptions, 1956–75

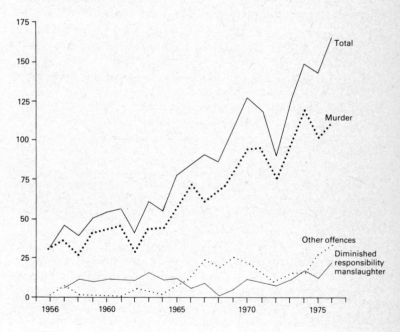

Note: The figure includes juveniles detained at Her Majesty's pleasure for an indeterminate period, but not men released on licence and subsequently recalled

Source: Sapsford and Banks (1979), Figure 3

FIGURE 2: The male life sentence population, 1957–77

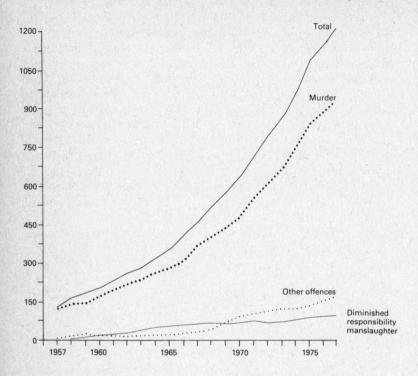

Note: The figures are for the first of January of each year. Juveniles detained for an indeterminate period are included, and also men transferred in from outside England and Wales, but not men released on licence and subsequently recalled

Source: Sapsford and Banks (1979), Figure 4

male lifers (including cases detailed 'during Her Majesty's Pleasure – offenders who were younger than eighteen at the time the offence was committed) grew from around thirty a year to well over one hundred and fifty, and the population from one hundred and thirty three at the beginning of 1957 to over twelve hundred in 1979. The scale of the increases is illustrated in Figures 1 and 2. As can be seen, a part of the increase in population is due to the offence of diminished-responsibility manslaughter created by Section 2 of the Homicide Act 1957, which appears to have recruited to the prison population cases who would previously have been found insane and committed to a mental hospital (see Gibson and Klein, 1969). Another part is contributed by substantial increases in the use of life sentences for offences other than homicide. Between 1941 and 1950 *at most* one life sentence was given each year on average, and not many more between 1951 and 1965, but in the period from 1966 to 1970 the annual average shot up to more than twenty, and the population grew from one man on 1 January 1941 to seven in 1956 and to over a hundred by the end of 1970. (The cause of this increased use is not clear. One suddenly begins to find life appearing as a penalty used in cases of arson from about 1964, and courts in the north of England tended not to give life sentences nearly as often as southern courts before about 1966, but the reasons for these changes in court policy are not at all clear.) Together, however, these two sources contribute only a quarter to the increases, the rest being due to the increased number of murderers now in prison.

A large part of this increase in the population of murderers has to be due to the abolition of capital punishment, for before abolition about two out of every three convicted murders (excluding those respited on grounds of insanity and transferred to Broadmoor) were hanged – a proportion which remains fairly constant back as far as the turn of the century (see Gower Commission, 1953). On the assumption that this proportion would have continued to be applied, one may calculate that more than half of the lifers now in prison would not now be alive at all. The assumption is a pure guess, for one cannot be sure that more than one hanging every week – which is what would now be involved, if receptions had risen at the rate which they in fact did – would be politically tolerable even if hanging were still in force. Be that as it may, there can be no doubt that *some* part of the increase is due to the Homicide Act 1957 (which abolished hanging for all except a very restricted category of offences) and the Murder (Abolition of Death Penalty) Act 1965 (which abolished all executions for a trial period only – abolition was not made permanent until December 1969). The rest – at least 20 per cent on any reasonable set of assumptions, and quite possibly more – is due to a genuine increase in murderers received.

The increase in murder receptions, which is at least partly responsible for the rise in population, dates from around the time when capital punishment was virtually abolished, so there is a temptation to argue a causal relationship between the two: that capital punishment was a deterrent and that its abolition has increased the incidence of murder. However, there is no evidence for such a proposition. Abolition has not historically been associated with a rise in the offence for which the death penalty was previously in force, and in other countries murder rates seem if anything to be higher in death-penalty than in abolitionist jurisdictions (see, for example Calvert, 1927; Gower Commission, 1953; Fattah, 1972; Bailey, 1974). One should note also that the type of offence which many who favour the reintroduction of capital punishment would wish to deter – murder for gain and in the course of theft – is *not* among the varieties showing the fastest rate of increases since 1956.

Early Home Office analyses carried out by the late Christopher Wallis in 1969 (reported in Sapsford and Banks, 1979) showed that reprieve from the death penalty was 'predictable' by the 'type' of the offence of which the man had been convicted and his reported mental state: reprieve was most common among men who killed members of their immediate family and among men whose records showed no reported mental disturbance, and least common among cases which contained theft or sexual molestation as a component or where the label of 'psychopath' had been applied. Subsequent analyses have shown that these factors are also associated with term served in prison before release on licence. Of men who killed their own or other people's children without any element of sexual molestation between 1956 and 1972, for example, only 15 per cent were still in prison eleven years after they had been sentenced. Of men who killed wives, girlfriends or men other than in the course of theft, 26 per cent were still inside at the end of their eleventh year, while of people who killed for sexual reasons or in the course of theft 60 per cent were still in prison. A different pattern is discernible in numbers *convicted* of murder year by year, however: since 1956 the fastest rate of increase has been in the murder of women for sexual reasons, the slowest for family killings, murders arising out of drunken quarrels and the 'sexual' killing of children, with the remainder (including the old 'capital' offences) somewhere in between.

2.2:   *Treatment policy and prison regime*

With lifers, questions of 'treatment' and 'management' are very much intertwined, for the prison authorities have the task of devising a lifestyle for a life-sentence prisoner which will 'serve him up' to the releasing authorities fresh and releasable at a time not of their choosing. Generally, in fact, the point comes substantially *after* the time when in their judgement he is likely to be in peak condition for release. They have the task, as they see it, of preserving him in reasonable condition during 'knock-back periods' when the releasing authorities have turned him down at review and also dealing with a few men whose release is certainly many more years in the future than would be true of the average case. As people differ, this tends to mean individualized planning.

The system had coped *ad hoc* with its few life-sentence prisoners in the 1960s, but by the middle 1970s the population had grown to the point where the authorities felt the need for a more carefully designated use of facilities and more 'manpower planning' in devising careers for lifers. A new system was therefore devised, using two large prisons as allocating and classifying centres feeding a range of training prisons from close-security category A establishments down through B and C to the category D open prisons (Leyhill and, later, Sudbury) so arranged that moves between prisons could be seen as progressive by the prisoner and that substantial populations in each prison (seldom fewer than thirty) would allow some expertise to build up among the staff without lifers coming to dominate the training prison. It was in one of the main allocation centres, just at the point of transition, that my research was carried out. This gave me a substantial population including men at all stages of sentence, as the new 'allocation period' cases were additional to an already extensive group of men who had often spent most of their life sentence to date in the one establishment.

The concept of prison as a form of treatment for offenders is a product of the twentieth century. In the nineteenth century prison was a deterrent, akin to the death penalty in that its aim was to prevent crime by instilling fear of consequences; 'insofar as the moral reform of the prisoners might be an aim (it was pursued) primarily through the discipline of punishment' (Home Office, 1950). By the turn of the century, however, reformers were arguing that prison should work towards the reform and rehabilitation of its inmates, and by the 1950s the Gower Commission was able to report that the old regime of isolation and deliberately irritating and degrading labour no longer existed and that current policy aimed towards useful and interesting work, education and communal leisure. Nonetheless the Commission raised the warning that:

> It is not easy to adapt the prisons of this country to the new ideas. Most were built under the old regime and their structure is dictated by it . . . They do not fit, either structurally or psychologically, with concepts of the purpose of imprisonment so different as those which prevail today.

The old prisons still exist; the one in which I did my fieldwork was built as a county gaol in the middle of the last century.

Work discipline and 'habits of industry' lie at the core of the Victorian notion of 'a good and useful life', and work in prison forms one of the major aspects of 'rehabilitative training'; it is stated policy that every prisoner must be found work to do in prison. At the same time, work is also considered a privilege, something that helps to make time pass in prison. (Thus we find the curious paradox in prison practice that men can be punished for not working but can also have work withdrawn from them as a punishment.) During the 1960s and early 1970s considerable reorganization of prison industries took place – partly to bring them into line with the kind of work that prisoners would be doing on release and partly to try and make some kind of profit for the government. In the 1950s virtually all prison work was devoted to the upkeep of prisons and the production of furniture and consumables for other government departments (Gower Commission, p. 221); by 1979, 20 per cent of industrial workshop output was work undertaken for outside sales (Home Office, 1980).

One should not overrate the scope and breadth of work in prison, however. In 1969, the Parole Board noted in their annual report:

> During our visits to prison we have seen men performing tasks that can hardly have any effect other than to depress and frustrate them . . . The Board therefore welcomes the plans to modernise prison industry. (Parole Board, 1970, p. 27)

However, over six thousand men in prison in 1979 were employed on domestic duties.

During 1968, as part of a review of educational facilities throughout custodial establishments, vocational training facilities were amalgamated with the education service. In that year seventy-eight courses catered for about thirteen hundred prisoners, the largest categories being brickwork and painting and decorating. Numbers on courses grew considerably during the early 1970s, particularly on the construction industries side. Various projects intermediate between work and training were also tried out: for example, a Braille transcription unit was opened in a young offender's prison in 1973, and another in 1974 in the prison where I did my fieldwork.

Formal education in custodial institutions ranges from casual 'evening classes' through extensive remedial work to 'O' and 'A' level classes and even degree-level work (through the Open University). It was estimated (Home Office, 1974) that some 65 per cent of the daily average population of prisons, remand centres, borstals and detention centres took advantage of one or another of these facilities – though the bulk are likely to have been in the last two types of institution, where many of the population are younger than the school leaving age. In general and higher education there has been a progressive raising of the Department's sights over time: in 1968, summarizing the position of the time, the Radzinowicz Committee noted only that 'In addition . . . there are special arrangements made for tutorials and correspondence courses for those willing and able to obtain GCE or other qualifications' (Advisory Council, 1968); by 1975 there had been one hundred and forty prisoners enrolled with the Open University, one hundred and seventy-three course examinations sat, one hundred and-fifty four passes and one man had graduated. The development of Open University work within prisons has been particularly important in the 'careers' of life-sentence prisoners, as we shall see.

Over all attempts to extend opportunities and facilities for life-sentence prisoners since the middle 1960s, however, has settled a dust cloud of increased concern with containment and the physical security of the prisons. Although few or none of the parties who helped to form policy on security and the prisons were aiming at a restriction of scope in the life-sentence regime, a succession of measures aimed at preventing escapes (and in large part escapes of men on long fixed terms, such as spies and train robbers, not lifers) succeeded during the 1970s in making prison greyer and more confining for all men serving long and/or indeterminate sentences. This factor, coupled with the apparently inevitable 'boarding school' regime of a total institution run on quasi-military lines, makes how the prisoner is actually treated difficult to conceptualize as 'treatment'.

Considering the life sentence within the prison context, it shares many characteristics with other sentences of similar length (the average lifer serves between nine and twelve years before release on licence). Facilities are available for medical and psychiatric treatment, for trade training and for basic or higher education; the educational facilities are particularly good in the prison where this project was carried out. In free time there are limited sports facilities, books, television and normal associational activities such as snooker and table tennis. There is work – though generally of an undemanding and repetitive nature – during the day. Lifers are exposed to the same kind of regime as other prisoners, with its extreme emphasis on routine, its requirement of obedience to prison officers and to rules laid down by others and its tendency to make the prisoner dependent on staff even for trivial facilities. They are housed, many of them, in the same noisy, over-crowded, depressing Victorian prisons of which a Minister of State at the Home Office said that:

> The statistics have little meaning until one has entered a small cell in one of our ancient fortress gaols and seen, and even smelled, the effect of these men living in an oppressive claustrophobic atmosphere. (Lord Harris, *The Guardian*, 8 November 1978)

Sex offenders may encounter great hostility from the other prisoners and be forced to ask for solitary confinement for their own protection, thereby 'voluntarily' impoverishing their daily lives still further, and others may have this impoverishment forced upon them from time to time in response to their unruly or uncooperative behaviour.

One day in prison is much like any other day, and all days are drab. I can do no better than to quote from *British Prisons* by Fitzgerald and Sim (1982), who have caught the drabness and indignity exactly:

> Each morning about six o'clock, and after the first count of the day, the cells are unlocked. In the next two hours, they 'slop out', wash, make their beds, clean the cells, and eat breakfast. 'Slopping out' is one of the most symbolic practices of modern life. Prisoners carry their piss-pots down the landing, and queue up to empty them in the recess . . . Razor blades are handed out and collected back each morning. If a prisoner wishes to grow or shave off a moustache he has to seek permission from the governors. Applications to see the governor, doctor or social worker must be made during this period. Applications are made through the principal officer, who decides whether or not a prisoner will see the governor. Before eight o'clock, prisoners who are going to workshops line up outside their cells. They are counted out of the wing, marched over to and counted out of the

workshop and marched back into the wing . . . for dinner. They
are counted again . . . (In the early afternoon) they line up for
work and are counted and marched back . . . When moving from
one part of the prison to another, prisoners are always escorted
and formally handed over to the officer in charge. After tea,
prisoners are . . . locked in their cells for a 'quiet hour', which is
historically provided as a space for personal reflection. It also
coincides with the time staff take tea. In the early evening,
prisoners may be unlocked for a recreation period, when they
can associate with others, attend evening classes, watch television, read papers, and play games such as darts, snooker,
chess and table tennis . . . The majority either stay in their cells,
watch television, or simply walk around the (wing) . . . talking
with friends . . . By about nine o'clock prisoners are back in their
cells . . . Officers begin to lock up, counting as they go from cell
to cell. About ten o'clock the lights go out. Throughout the
night, the patrolling officer will look through the peep-hole
of each cell to check that the occupants are inside and asleep.
For top security prisoners, the cell light burns all night.
(pp. 65–7)

With minor variations of detail this was the routine of the
prison in which my research was carried out. However, some
people might escape some of its tedium some of the time: certain
prison jobs meant being out of the cell at times when others
were 'banged up', and 'red-band status' – a privilege to be
earned – entitled prisoners to move around the prison without
an escort on legitimate errands. The majority of lifers were in
single cells, but there were a few 'dormitories' – larger cells
housing three men – occupied by men early in sentence.

The prisoner may adapt to the detailed indignities of daily
prison life, but the key elements of vulnerability, secrecy and
suspicion remain throughout sentence. Everything which the
prisoner does is open to inspection and interpretation. His cell is
searched periodically; he is under observation most of the time
that he is out of it; his behaviour is seen as symptomatic of
mental condition – choosing to stay in the cell during association time, for example, may be 'withdrawn behaviour'. Almost
anything he wants – extra writing paper, a book, his light on for
an extra half hour in the evening – needs an officer's permission
(which would generally be granted, but this does not alter the
fact that it needs to be sought). A 'master–slave' mentality
grows up, with officers afraid that prisoners' good behaviour
may be 'manipulative' and prisoners dependent for a reason-

able life on the goodwill and tolerance of particular officers. Even their love letters will be read by officers and perhaps rejected for rewriting because of 'offensive language' or because they comment on prison conditions. Incoming letters may be stopped for a variety of reasons – sometimes without the prisoner even knowing of the letter's existence – or news of personal tragedies may be 'broken' to the prisoner by a paternalistic third party such as a probation officer.

All this the lifer shares with other prisoners. The main difference is the indeterminacy of the sentence: 'fixed term' men have a degree of uncertainty because of parole, but no lifer knows exactly when he will be released, or whether he will be released at all. For most, release at around the tenth year is a reasonable expectation, but there can be no certainty and some men (particularly those who committed sexual offences) can expect to serve most of the rest of their lives in prison, while still hoping from year to year. Here again the keynotes are vulnerability, secrecy and suspicion. Release on licence is ultimately the task of the Home Secretary, advised by a group of senior officials in the Home Office, very few of whom will ever have met a life-sentence prisoner. (There is no *unconditional* release for lifers; they are liable to be recalled to prison at any time during the rest of their lives, for committing another offence or even for non-criminal but 'ominous' behaviour.) Since the Parole Board was set up in the late 1960s every case has been considered by them. They have an effective power of veto on release: they cannot compel release on the Home Secretary, but he may not release against their advice (except through the medium of a Royal Pardon). Both in turn are advised by central divisions in Prison Department and the main Home Office, who draw on reports made at the time of the trial plus current reports from prison governors, assistant governors, medical officers, prison probation officers, prison psychologists, perhaps education officers, perhaps visiting psychotherapists etc., chaplains and the different prison officers who supervise each aspect of the prisoner's life. The prisoner is also interviewed and reported on by the prison's Local Review Committee. Except in rare cases prisoners are not considered until their seventh year, but thereafter they come up for review every year or two until the decision is made to release them – though in recent years the review of 'hard core' cases has often been put off.

The consequences of the nature of the sentence and of the way in which it is administered are threefold:

1. The prisoner can have no certain knowledge of when he will be released but is continually stimulated to hope for release by the review procedures.
2. He cannot influence those in whose hands his life lies – the staff around him can affect his future but not decide it, and this means also that they cannot make and keep promises to him.
3. By the same token, he can have no entirely open friendships with any member of the prison staff, whether their employment be as discipline staff, administrators, teachers, work supervisors, social workers, doctors or psychologists, because all staff may be writing reports about him.

He must also watch his behaviour at all times. Anything he does may count as a symptom: if he makes friends with prisoners he may be 'mixing with the subversives', but if he avoids making friends he may be 'withdrawn'. Moreover, for any infraction of rules he may be punished twice – once at the disciplinary hearing, and again (and again, and again) when he comes up for review. It would not seem unfair, on the face of it, to characterize the life-sentence prisoner as helpless in a world of nightmare uncertainties. It was the known psychological effects of helplessness and uncertainty which provided the focus for the quantitative side of the current research.

2.3:   *Effects of long sentences: a summary of research*

One overwhelming fear of long-term prisoners, well documented by Cohen and Taylor in the passage quoted in Chapter 1, is that one will in some sense 'deteriorate' in prison, that it is necessary to struggle in order to preserve oneself. Rasch (1977) reports that 62 per cent of a sample of lifers he had interviewed experienced fears of going insane at some time during the sentence. Serge (1970, p. 58) speaks of: '. . . a state of vegetative slow motion existence in which sharp sufferings and sharp joys no longer play a part.' Ward and Kassebaum (1971) have found the same reaction in women's prisons: '. . . you lose the power, if you're not careful, to make even a small decision, or to harbour an original thought.' I received similar comments in my own preliminary discussions with prisoners and staff, and staff made similar reports to the Advisory Council on the Penal System (1968).

To some extent the findings of research workers suggest factual grounding for such fears. Silverman *et al* (1966) have duplicated in samples of newly-received and longer-serving prisoners the perceptual differences which are observable between schizophrenics of differently constricted personal styles and between schizophrenics and normals. Sluga (1977) claims to have found by clinical examination what he terms a 'functional psychosyndrome' typical of men serving long sentences who have been inside for four or six years, comprising 'psychic anaesthesia', disturbed comprehension, impoverished ability to relate and increased isolation consequent on increased extraversion. The clinical work is backed up by more systematic cross-sectional testing using the MMPI (Minnesota Multiphasic Personality Inventory) and tests of motor ability and concentration. The last two of these register a decline in ability over time. The MMPI suggests that neurotic personality defences diminish with increased imprisonment, being replaced by defences involving an apparent 'loss of reality' more characteristic of schizoid personalities. He notes also large depressive reactions, frequently with hypochondriac features.

Hautaluona and Scott (1973) and Tokuyama *et al* (1973) in Japan note that men well advanced in life sentences seem to be more homogeneous and have 'flatter' personalities than others. Terence and Pauline Morris (1961, 1963) found, even in the course of a relatively short period in a prison for short-term men,

> . . . several prisoners on the downhill path, men who made a joke less and less, whose appearance became increasingly untidy and who became progressively disinterested in everything about them . . .

though they point out that in all of these cases there were severe personality problems already in existence. Taylor (1961) describes such cases – though he found only a handful during several years as a prison psychologist – and also reports a decline in performance intelligence discovered in a small-scale study of shorter term prisoners.

However, other studies give a picture so much less extreme that it barely amounts to measurable deterioration. Smith and his colleagues at Durham University carried out extensive cross-sectional testing of the intelligence, personality and attitudes of two hundred long-term prisoners; the results are reported in Banister *et al* (1973), Heskin *et al* (1973, 1974), and

Bolton *et al* (1976). Briefly, there are four main strands to the research:

1. The investigators looked for measurable signs of cognitive deterioration; such deterioration has been reported from mental hospitals in a number of studies, from concentration camps by Kral *et al* (1967), and among very small samples of prisoners by Taylor (1961). Comparing four groups of prisoners sentenced to ten years or more divided on the basis of their total length of previous imprisonment (from none to forty years), the investigators found no decline in general intelligence as measured by the WAIS (Wechsler Adult Intelligence Scale). Indeed, there was some improvement on one of the test's subscales, though there was some evidence of psychomotor decline over and above the effects of ageing.

2. The subjects completed an extensive battery of pencil-and-paper 'personality' tests. The main findings were a decrease in extraversion with length of imprisonment and an increase in hostility (particularly self-directed hostility).

3. Semantic-differential techniques showed a lower self-evaluation in men who had served longer. This was interpreted as a possible increasing equation of 'self' with the concept 'prisoner', which is held in low esteem by all groups.

4. Follow-up testing was carried out some nineteen months later, and the results were compared with those obtained over the same period from a non-prisoner control group. During this period the prisoners showed, if anything, an improvement in IQ relative to the controls, this being mainly due to improved scores on the verbal scales of the test. The finding of psychomotor impairment was not duplicated – which would indeed hardly have been expected over such a short period. There were changes in 'personality' scores between test and retest, but these are interpreted by the authors as being due partly to lowered test anxiety at the second visit and partly to the selection effect caused by the paroling of some of the more 'mature' men during the period between test and retest.

Goemann (1977), in a clinical survey of German 'lifers', found no observable deterioration even after twenty years inside. Another German study reported by Rasch (1977, 1981), using medical examination, intelligence tests, semantic differentials, interview assessment and a variety of questionnaires (including the MMPI and Cattell's 16 Personality Factor Questionnaire) also found no systematic evidence of deterioration, or of any marked change except greater feelings of guilt. Depression was noted frequently in the interview assessment for men who had served long terms, but it was also fairly common among more recently received men. None of this adds up to a marked deterioration. Indeed, Rasch comments with some surprise on how well the lifers whom he studied adapted to the outside world after release.

The position is thus somewhat confused. On balance, the fact of imprisonment would appear not to make dramatic changes in self-esteem over and above those already brought about by self-labelling; but extended terms of imprisonment appear likely to lead to depression of self-image.

Indeterminacy would appear a particular strong source of anxieties and feelings of powerlessness. It is a source of anxiety even for borstal boys. For the man serving a long 'fixed' term of imprisonment, parole may be the most disturbing feature of the system if he has any belief that its outcome can be affected by any of his actions. Among men who opt out of parole altogether, a majority give low expectation of being released and the general stress of the selection process as their reasons – uncertainty, the 'wind-up' involved in building up one's hopes, and the consequent disappointment and depression when one is turned down (Nuttall *et al*, 1977, Chapter 4).

For lifers, whose sentence is utterly indeterminate except for a vague knowledge of the 'average sentence', everything that one does may be judged by the authorities as of relevance to the question of release. Alternatively, it can turn planning into a senseless activity;

> . . . a life sentence has no fixed length you see, it's an indefinite period, so there's no point in making plans of any sort for going out. I don't even know if I am going to be let out, never mind when. So for instance a word like 'tomorrow' doesn't have any meaning to me except in the way that tomorrow might be my day for having a bath . . .   (a murderer quoted in Parker, 1973, p. 20)

Summarizing the general drift of this discussion, one would have to say that the research evidence to date is patchy, inconclusive and on occasions contradictory. Descriptive writers appear convinced that prison has longer-term effects. Staff claim to have observed deterioration in prisons and the prisoners themselves appear very much afraid that they too will deteriorate without knowing that they have done so. However, the formal research evidence is very mixed. Some studies find psychological and behavioural deficits which they identify as effects of time spent in prison; others fail to identify such changes. On the whole the second group are more convincing by their scope and methodology, and at best the case must be considered not proven.

3

THE LIFER PROJECT I –
reactions to imprisonment

Although the research evidence on prisons, taken as a whole, provides at best ambiguous support for the occurrence of deterioration in prisons, prisoners themselves certainly believe that people deteriorate in the course of long and indeterminate sentences and prison staff share this belief. If one believes at all that the environment affects behaviour and mentation, one would surely expect some effect from the changed life circumstances of the prisoner and the depriving and controlling regime which he is forced to undergo. This chapter describes a research project to examine such effects.

3.1: *The theoretical base of the project*

Deterioration as a result of confinement and loss of freedom of action certainly appears to occur in other types of institution and other situations of deprivation, to judge from the research literature. Studies of the effects of psychiatric hospitals on those who are confined in them (e.g. Martin, 1955; Belknap, 1956; Barton, 1959; Ellenberger, 1960; Wing, 1962; Wing and Brown, 1970; Shiloh, 1971) describe a condition which they variously term 'institutionalization', 'institutionalism' or 'institutional neurosis'. There are parallel accounts from 'ordinary' hospitals (Titmuss, 1958). The condition is characterized by apathy and reduced motivation coupled with extreme dependency on routine and the support of the institution. It is generally attributed to the administrative effects of the institution: all the 'rewards' are for quiet, resigned, cooperative and settled behaviour, so that such behaviour becomes habitual to the point where the man becomes too passive to present problems.

The condition may be seen as rendering the man unfit for outside life; Wing (1962), for example, found that patients gradually become indifferent to events outside the hospital. Shiloh's 1971 paper reports on five hundred and sixty mental patients in one hospital, at least 40 per cent of whom did not want to leave. He characterizes this group as passive and silent, given to rambling or disjointed answers, quick to lapse into apathy or non-cooperation; they consider the hospital as a substitute for an old folks' home, being well aware of its loneliness and negative emotional aspects but putting up with these for the sake of its meagre comforts.

Some degree of withdrawal and apathy appears to have been common in the wartime concentration camps and to have mediated survival in the early stages. The facility for insulating oneself by coming to feel temporarily that 'I'm not here' or 'this is not happening to me' or by replacing the 'I who feels' by the 'I who observes' was sometimes effective in shielding the prisoner from complete and devastating shock; many cases are given by Bettelheim (1943, 1960), and at second hand by Dimsdale (1974) and Nardini (1952). However, as a permanent strategem withdrawal was most invariably fatal.

> The final and most complete state of withdrawal was . . . the 'Musselmann' stage . . . characterised by profound apathy, complete indifference to the surroundings and a lack of any response to the environment, both physical and interpersonal. Almost all who reached this stage and were not immediately rescued by their comrades never returned to it. They were immediately selected out and killed.   (Dimsdale, 1974)

> Prisoners entered the Musselmann stage when emotion could no longer be evoked in them. For a time they fought for food, but after a few weeks even that stopped . . . in the last, just before the terminal stage, they no longer ate . . .   (Bettelheim, 1960, p. 155–6)

Bettelheim characterizes these 'muslims' as:

> . . . prisoners who came to believe the repeated statements of the guards – that there was no hope for them and that they would never leave the camp except as corpses – who came to feel that their environment was one over which they could exercise no influence whatsoever.   (1960, p. 151)

The almost inevitable association of death with such depressions when they occurred in the camps, unless other prisoners intervened, is also noted by Nardini (1952). Greenson (1949) reports on similar but considerably less extreme cases, observed among repatriated prisoners of war, of apathy so strong that it is readily confusable with schizophrenia.

Confinement *per se* is not required for this kind of disturbance to be manifested. Apathy, listlessness and loss of 'grasp on the world' are reported for Africans in South Africa whose villages have been uprooted (Nadine Gordimer, cited in Chapter 2 of Cohen and Taylor, 1972), in villages which have been struck by mass unemployment (Jahoda *et al*, 1972; Jahoda, 1982) and form the mainstay of news reports on political refugees and persons displaced by physical disasters. The linking feature in all these circumstances would appear to be the sudden loss of control over the environment and over the course of one's life. In most of them a similar time-course may be discerned, with initial frenetic activity – aimed at finding some way to cope – giving way to apathy, withdrawal and self-perceived helplessness as the circumstance proved truly beyond the person's power of coping.

A key notion in the discussion which follows will be the concept of 'expectancy'. Men's psychological reactions to the conditions of imprisonment will obviously depend very much on what they had expected, and they come in with very different expectations. To put this another way, the effects of deprivation of liberty or of control depend on one's prior motivation towards controlling one's reinforcement. A number of writers have suggested that many of the choices a man makes in prison, as to how he is to deal with his sentence and what use he should make of facilities offered by the authorities, can be attributed to the culture, habits and aspirations which he brings with him into prison. Prisoners of different social classes, educational levels and previous experiences may come into prison with different expectations of the role of the prisoner, and staff's differential perception of them and their attitudes will also affect how they are treated.

One example of such varied expectancy at work is given by Tittle (1972) in his description of a therapeutic institution some of whose inmates were voluntary patients while others were committed there by the criminal justice system. He found that perceived deprivation was much more salient in determining the mode of socialization than was actual deprivation. Those inmates who saw themselves as 'prisoners' and formed something of an inmate subculture gave restriction of liberty as the aspect of the regime which made them take this stance; those who saw themselves as 'patients', on the other hand, gave the large amount of freedom they experienced as the reason. Prior expectation of how much freedom to expect made some see the institution as a prison by comparison with their expectations, while others saw it as a hospital. To some extent the attitude adopted was independent of legal status: there were voluntary patients who saw themselves as prisoners and actual prisoners who saw themselves as patients.

A general theory of behaviour as determined by expectation of being in control ('locus of control of reinforcement') has been put forward by Rotter and his colleagues (see Chapter 1 of Rotter *et al*, 1972, for an outline). The theory is concerned, among other things, with the notion of generalized expectancies – whether the subject expects in general to control his or her own reinforcements, and therefore takes responsibility for outcome, or whether he or she 'places' control predominantly in the external world. A wide range of predictions about the relationship of locus of control to social circumstances have been made and confirmed: class, race, sex and nationality all affect (or fail to affect) perceived locus of control according to the real extent of the subjects' personal power. (See Battle and Rotter, 1963; Lefcourt and Ladwig, 1965; Parsons *et al*, 1970; Reitz and Groff, 1972; McGinnies *et al*, 1974; Malikiosi and Ryckman, 1977; Aberbach, 1977.) There is also a substantial literature on perceived locus of control as a trait of personality (for reviews see Lefcourt, 1966, 1976; Rotter *et al*, 1972).

In studying putative effects of imprisonment and indeterminacy, however, we are concerned with hopelessness about control not as a personality variable or the reaction to a long-running social/cultural situation but with more immediate effects of the constraining environment, and environmental effects on behaviour have been a close concern of the one kind of psychologist for virtually the whole history of the discipline. Learning theorists since before the turn of the century have studied what is called 'operant conditioning', the learning of voluntary responses which can be improved by reward or decreased by punishment – as opposed, for example to the eye-blink reflex, which is not under the subject's control. (Learning of responses involving involuntary behaviour is more the subject of 'classical' conditioning.) Operant conditioning is the study of responses made in order to control the environment – to avoid pain, for example, or to obtain a reward such as food.

The basic characteristic of this kind of learning is that the experimental subject – whether rat or man – is in a position to learn that the outcome is to some extent under his control. He will always, (or sometimes, in the case of partial reinforcement) obtain the reward Y or escape the pain, if he makes the desired response X. He can also learn that X does *not* lead to Y – that the response which typically preceded Y in the past has now ceased to do so. The number of responses he makes in vain before 'ceasing to bother' is related to the amount of information needed for such a decision to be reached; under past continuous reinforcement, when every response produced the reward, sometimes only a few trials will suffice to convince the subject that the connection is broken, while under partial reinforcement the subject is used to failure on some trials and may take a lot of 'convincing' that his response no longer produces the reward.

Interesting things happen, however, when an aversive outcome is no longer contingent on the reward – when whether or not the animal is given electric shock is entirely independent of his responding. These have been elucidated at length by Seligman and his colleagues; most of the history of the research is summarized in Seligman (1975). The typical experiment is described in pages 25–6 of Seligman's 1975 book. In these 'triadic' experiments three groups are used. The first receive experience of 'controllability' of the aversive stimulus: they are restrained in a hammock and given shocks, but they can turn these off by some response – generally by pressing a panel with their noses. A second group are 'yoked' to the first; similarly restrained, they receive exactly the same incidence and duration of shock as the first group but have no control at all over it – no response of theirs will turn the shock off. A third group is restrained but received no shocks; in some experiments they are not even restrained. When tried out in the shuttle-box twenty-four hours later, groups one and three mostly have no difficulty in learning to escape shock, but the yoked group mostly fail to escape altogether and those that do escape tend to be much slower at learning to do so – though all show evidence of considerable distress, particularly at first. Seligman calls the phenomenon 'learned helplessness'. Similar results are reported for other species and other apparatus or settings. Later work (Maier *et al*, 1972; Seligman *et al*, 1971) has shown that the situation extends beyond simple escape responses; while responses which are instinctive or well learned are not necessarily disrupted, active problem-solving may very often be impaired.

An even more striking variant of the basic triadic experiment was carried out by Maier (1970). The above design was used, except that in group one the dogs were trained to *refrain* from responding. Instead of being able to turn off the shock by operant response, their heads were closely surrounded with sensitive panels and they learned that shock could be terminated only by keeping the head very still and not touching the panels. Again the yoked group received the same incidence and duration of shock but had no way of controlling it, and again learned helplessness was found in the yoked group but not in either of the others. What appeared to have happened was not just that the dogs had learned that making an operant response terminated shock; they had learned, in contradistinction to group two, that shock can be *under their control*.

Central to the interpretation of all these result as put forward by Seligman and his co-workers is the assumption that an organism is capable of learning that outcome is independent of response in a given situation. This would seem a fairly obvious proposition to common sense, but it has caused difficulty for learning theorists because it appears to involve propositional learning (learning 'that X is the case') rather than simply behavioural learning (learning 'to press the bar for food'). However, it is essential for even the simplest theory of operant conditioning; in learning that pressing the bar produces food, the rat has also to learn that other responses – wiggling its tail, for example – have no effect. That an integration over time and an inference about probabilities are involved should worry learning theorists no more than they do in the case of partial reinforcement. Nonetheless, learned helplessness is an essentially *cognitive* theory, rather than just a branch of simple learning theory: it is the subject's *expectancy*, rather than simple exposure, which defines the situation.

Many of the 'learned helplessness' results hold true for men as well. Hiroto (1974), for example, duplicated the basic triadic experiments using college students as subjects and loud noises as aversive stimulus. When subjects were tested later, using a finger shuttle-box in which subjects could escape the noise by moving their hands from one side to the other, the 'yoked' subjects failed to avoid the noise; for the most part they sat passively and accepted it. Glass and Singer (1972), in a similar design, found that control over loud and irritating noise (or even mere belief in control) averted the defect in proof-reading shown by those who experienced it as uncontrollable. Students who had previously been given unsolvable discrimination problems showed fewer competitive plays in a subsequent 'prisoner's dilemma' game. Adult subjects exposed to uncontrollable noise show subsequent selective interference with the learning process – their rating of their likelihood of success in the next trial of a task presented as requiring skill was almost unaffected by success or failure in previous trials, though this did not hold for a task where chance was presented as the main factor. Seligman's interpretation of this finding parallels Brickman's explanation of a rather similar phenomenon:

> Learned helplessness produces a cognitive set in which people believe that success and failure is independent of their own skilled actions, and they therefore have difficulty learning that responses work.

Geer *et al* (1970) report results indicating that perception of control over aversive stimulation, even if non-veridical, can affect even autonomic responding. Other studies demonstrating performance deficit include Richter (1957), Dweck and Repucci (1973), Fosco and Geer (1971) and Lubow *et al* (1982). However, there appear to be circumstances under which the basic 'learned helplessness' paradigm does not fit the facts with humans, and we shall be examining these further below under the heading of 'Reactance'.

The relevance of the task during which helplessness is 'established' to the subsequent test condition obviously affects the extent of performance deficit in humans. The interaction of task-relevance and prior expectancy, is elucidated by the results of a study carried out by Brickman *et al* (1976). Ninety-six high school students were given a symbol discrimination test preceded by a carefully manipulated feedback from other tests designed to give the impression that the subject had succeeded or failed and that these earlier tests were or were not predictive of performance on the final test – in other words whether they were relevant or irrelevant. Subjects had already been divided into those who expected to succeed and those who did not. The two main findings were (1) that relevant success was more effective than irrelevant success in improving performance, and (2) that while relevant success was the factor most likely to improve performance among those of high expectancy, irrelevant failure had more effect than relevant success among those of low expectancy. The first of these two effects illustrates the effect of expectancy – prior success improves performance, while failure depresses it. The second is seen as the outcome of defensive attribution, relevant success being rejected by low expectancy subjects (attributed to chance) because accepting it would commit the subject to the belief that he or she could succeed again in the future, while irrelevant failure might even undermine the low expectancy to some extent. Studies by Mettee (1971) and Maracek and Mettee (1972) show that low-expectancy individuals do indeed tend to reject relevant success (and only relevant success). Predictability is another facet of the experience which influences the result: predictable events cause less helplessness than unpredictable ones (Seligman, 1968; Seligman and Meyer, 1970; Price and Geer, 1972). Seligman (1975, pp. 112 ff) argues that when an aversive event is predictable one has a safety signal: one at least knows when it will *not* occur.

An alternative theory about what happens when one's control of events is threatened or one's freedom circumscribed has been put forward by Brehm and his colleagues (see e.g. Wicklund, 1974): that one becomes motivationally aroused (which process is called 'reactance') to try to restore the freedom. This theory leads to predictions opposite to those of Seligman and his colleagues in the 'learned helplessness' situation, for whose validity some evidence has been offered. With human subjects, some experiments which set out to demonstrate learned helplessness in fact found that the supposedly 'helpless' group initiated more controlling behaviour than the other subjects; see for example, Roth and Bootzin (1974), Krantz and Glass (cited in Roth, 1980). A range of experiments have demonstrated that perception of 'alien control' or censorship motivates subjects to reassert their own freedom of choice in proportion to the importance of the freedom which is threatened. (See e.g. Hammock and Brehm, 1966; Brehm and Sensenig, 1966; Brehm *et al*, 1966; Mischel and Masters, 1966.)

The experimental evidence which supports 'reactance' has been ingeniously integrated with the 'learned helplessness' material in a paper by Wortman and Brehm (1975). Reactance, they suggest, should occur when subjects are exposed to uncontrollable outcome only if they had expected to have some control over the outcome and even then only to the extent that the outcome is important to the subject. A small amount of helplessness training is experienced by the subject as a threat to his freedom, and he reacts to restore his sense of freedom by showing that he is not helpless (i.e., performing better). A greater amount of helplessness training, however, convinces him of his helplessness. How quickly he is convinced depends in part on the importance of the outcome to him – how much freedom is threatened. It will depend also on how strongly he expected to control the outcome – because he has prior experience of control, because he knows that others similar to him have control, because he has expended a great deal of effort, or for a variety of other reasons. (As in the learned helplessness experiments, failure at a task is to be interpreted as loss of control.)

Wortman and Brehm cite Seligman's findings concerning 'immunization from helplessness' as confirmatory evidence of this interpretation: animals whose expectation of control is raised by prior controllable experience do not become helpless when presented with inescapable shock; moreover, their (futile) responses during the inescapable shock are far more numerous than those of 'unimmunized' animals. Another of Seligman's experiments (Seligman and Groves, 1970) extends this point; cage-raised dogs (who would presumably have a lower expectation of control, because they have not had to fend for themselves) were given two to four sessions of helplessness training before testing in the shuttle-box, and so were a group of mongrels. The cage-raised dogs were much likelier than the mongrels to show helplessness after two training sessions, thus confirming that past experience of control affects the likelihood of becoming helpless; however, after four sessions there was no difference between the two groups, perhaps confirming that the difference is one of degree only.

Experiments on human subjects add further support to the Wortman and Brehm synthesis. For example, Shaban and Welling (see Glass and Singer, 1972, pp. 122–30) forced subjects into completing a lengthy questionnaire twice. In one condition this was because the assistant said it had not been completed to her satisfaction, and in the other because of 'departmental rules'; thus some of the subjects had twice as much work as they had expected because they lost a battle of will with someone who was physically present and the others because of something entirely outside their (and her) control. The former group of subjects behaved more negatively and cheated where possible in a subsequent task – reactance was aroused by failure in a situation where control might be expected, but not in one where it was not expected.

So far we have considered two lines of theory and experimental evidence about how people react to circumstances which are unpleasant and are seen as threatening: constraints on freedom or disconfirmation of expectations about the self. On the one hand the individual may be goaded into fighting back against the constraint (*reactance*); on the other, he or she may come to doubt the ability to control and lapse into depressed passivity (*learned helplessness*). Both are seen as affected by the importance of the freedom or the belief, and in their behavioural consequences both are affected by the relevance or similarity of the constraining circumstance to the current situation. Both are essentially cognitive theories; the effects are produced not by mere exposure to a situation, but by the expectations of success or freedom of action which the individual brings into the situation.

An important concept for the integration of the two theories is the notion that expectations may be hierarchically ordered with respect to one another. The learned helplessness experiments on humans have mostly been concerned with fairly trivial performance tasks and the reactance experiments with fairly trivial limitations on choice. Both theories are ultimately concerned with more profound and disturbing threats to choice and competence, however. It is no more true that a subject has a single level of expectation than that he or she has a single goal. Goals are multiple – to do well in test 1, to do well in test 2, to do well in examinations, to succeed in general – and each has its associated level of expectation. Moreover, some goals (and expectancies) are subordinate to others: 'doing well in test 1' is one aspect of 'doing well in examinations', which in turn is only one aspect of 'succeeding in general'.

In the example, 'succeeding in general' is a crucial notion for understanding the literature on learned helplessness, reactance and locus of control. There is at the summit of the goal hierarchy a single superordinate goal of 'maintaining one's freedom of action', or 'succeeding', with an associated expectancy of succeeding or controlling one's own reinforcement, to which all other goals relate and which informs all other expectancies. The subject has a general 'picture' of his capabilities and his scope for action which is central to his life; it represents the limits of his aspirations and his whole knowledge of his place in the world. This picture is jealously guarded.

Now we should note that learned helplessness includes an important affective or emotional aspect, as well as the cognitive and motivational components which have already been discussed. Monkeys trained to feed in response to a signal and then presented with a fear-arousing stimulus during feeding showed dramatic signs of emotional disturbance, but these are not present in the case of animals who have been taught to actuate devices controlling the feeder; these, as their hunger increases, begin to make attempts to re-explore the operation of the switches (Masserman, 1943). Gatchel *et al* (1975) showed a high association in human subjects between self-report depression, anxiety, general emotionality and pre-treatment with inescapable aversive stimulation. We are also reminded that Pavlov called the result of over-hard discrimination tasks for dogs 'experimental neurosis' because of its affective content (see also Maier *et al*, 1969, for a fuller discussion).

Seligman has pointed out the remarkably close similarity between the laboratory phenomenon of learned helplessness and the clinical phenomenon of reactive depression, and there is a wealth of other evidence linking depression with belief in one's incompetence and impotence coupled with hopelessness for improvement in the future (see, for example, Beck, 1967; Beck *et al*, 1974; Lichtenberg, 1957; Melges and Bowlby, 1969; Abramson *et al*, 1978b). Seligman notes a considerable similarity or parallelism between the symptoms of the one as seen in the laboratory and the manifestations of the other in clinical practice, and between the cures of the two conditions. He lists some of the eliciting conditions of reactive depression – failure at work or school, death of a loved one, rejection by or separation from friends or loved ones, physical disease, financial difficulties, being faced with insoluble problems, growing old – and suggests that the linking factor is powerlessness and the experience of one's own actions is futile. Beck's description (1967, pp. 256–257) might be seen as illustration:

> The depressed patient is particularly sensitive to impediments to his goal-directed activity. An obstacle is regarded as an impossible barrier. Difficulty in dealing with a problem is interpreted as a total failure . . .

Of note also is the fact that those with an external locus of control are more prone to depression (Abramowitz, 1969; Goss and Morosko, 1970). This hopelessness can utterly sap the will to live: epidemics of suicide under hopeless conditions are described, for example, by Melges and Weisz (1971), and cases of 'natural death' which amount to giving up the will to live are discussed by Richter (1957), Seligman (1975) and Lefcourt (1976). At a more trivial level, Wener and Rehm (1975) have shown that mild depression ensues even in unimportant laboratory tasks, when feedback is 'rigged' to show an artificially low success rate – subjects with low-success feedback showed greater depression on a questionnaire measure, less self-report confidence and longer latencies of response.

Most depressives exhibit depression *per se* and also anxiety, but these two are separable, at least conceptually, in terms of whether expectations are actually disconfirmed or only under attack. Let us consider 'anxiety' as the painful experience of having one's higher-order expectancies threatened by events: anxiety results from a discrepancy between current or anticipated experience and any expectancy; and the amount of anxiety depends on the place of the expectancy in the hierarchy. 'Depression', following Seligman, may be seen as the experience of having to lower one's highest expectancies – of learning that outcome is independent of responding, that one cannot succeed, that one is not as competent as one thought. The case for this assertion will be argued later but we may note now that aversive situations produce fear for as long as uncertainty exists, but once the outcome is certainly uncontrollable this is replaced by passivity and depression. For example, when an infant monkey is separated from its mother it shows panic reactions at first – frantic activity and vocalization. If the mother is not returned, however, the monkey eventually curls up in a ball and just lies there, whining. (See, for example, Hartlow *et al*, 1970). Where fires and the like break out in theatres, the first reaction of the audience is to rush for the door in an obvious panic, but if it becomes apparent that there is no escape, calmness and resignation usually supervene (Quarantelli, 1954).

The difference between 'anxiety' and 'depression' (based respectively on uncertainty and hopelessness) is demonstrated in an example from Grinker and Spiegel (1945, p. 132): airmen in the middle of a tour of duty adopt a fatalistic attitude which '. . . is actually closer to a marked depression than a successful adaptation, but it does protect the individual against anxiety.' This begins to break down towards the end of the tour, when the airman's hopes for survival are more realistic, and intense anxiety may supervene. The distinction is well expressed in more psychoanalytic terms by Bibring (1953, p. 40):

> ... according to the viewpoint adopted here, *depression represents a*
> *basic reaction* to situations of narcissistic frustration which to
> prevent appears to be beyond the power of the ego, just as *anxiety*
> *represents a basic reaction* of the ego to situations of danger.

Depression in this sense is almost never seen in its pure form,
where hope has vanished totally, except in very extreme
circumstances – the *Musselmanner* described by Bettelheim
(1960), for instance, who became utterly apathetic and died not
long after. Normally, depression is mixed with anxiety. Utter
hopelessness about one's competence would lead almost inevitably to death. What happens more usually is that one is forced
to revise one's expectancies downwards but remains uncertain
how far downwards it is necessary to go. The whole framework
of the subject's life is disturbed. In the past, knowing his level of
competence, he knew which situations were 'safe'. Now he
'knows' he is less competent (or less lovable, or less admirable)
than he thought, but he does not know how much less; new
situations, and even some thoroughly familiar ones, become
tests and threats. Thus depression as normally experienced
consists in lowered expectancy plus anxiety about having to
lower it still further; only 'when the bottom has been reached'
will the anxiety disappear.

The course of fear and anxiety as one becomes more
experienced with and knowledgeable about the fear-producing
stimulus has been charted, in a detailed comparison of novice
parachutists with men who had made over a hundred jumps, by
Epstein and Fenz (Epstein and Fenz, 1965; Epstein 1967; Fenz
and Epstein, 1967). When asked to rate their own fear on a
scale, novices and experienced men show quite different patterns. For novices the rating climbs steadily from the night
before, through reaching the airport and boarding the aircraft,
to a peak at the 'ready for jump' signal; it then declines steadily
through waiting to jump, jumping, and the chute opening. For
the experienced man the peak comes very early, in the night
before the jump; from there it declines steadily to the jump
itself, then rises steadily to and through the chute opening. The
difference reflects a combination of commitment and
knowledge. The novice is uncertain whether he will actually
dare to jump right up to the point when the 'ready' signal
occurs; he then realizes he will be able to do so, and anxiety
diminishes. For the experienced man, the point of highest
uncertainty is before the morning of the jump, when he is not

sure whether it will occur (because of weather conditions, for instance). Once he is sure the jump will occur, anxiety diminishes to the actual jump (the last point at which his fate is entirely under his control) but rises again after he has jumped, reflecting his greater knowledge of what can go wrong on the way down. Epstein (1967), discussing these and other data, describes anxiety as a state of undirected arousal following perception of danger, as opposed to fear, and ties the distinction to uncertainty about the outcome and how one may affect it.

Anxiety, then, is the product of a perceived imbalance between expectation and outcome in a situation where the goal is valued; this class of situations will include all failures attributable to the agent, as they all reflect ultimately on the basic expectation for freedom/success. The imbalance is corrected, and the anxiety cured, by changing one or more of the terms 'result', 'expectation', 'goal', or 'value' in this equation. One may attempt to deal directly with the feeling of anxiety, decoupling it from the goal with which it is associated and treating it not as a state of expectation but as a 'thing' in its own right – by trying solutions which have reduced anxiety in the past (e.g., alcohol or compulsive eating) or by suppressing it altogether. An example of the latter tactic is given by Fenz and Epstein (1967), who found that novice parachutists who felt fear on the day of the jump refused to associate this fear with parachuting – fear appears in responses to TAT (Thematic Apperception Test) pictures of neutral scenes but not of scenes of parachuting. One may change the goal – sublimation, the replacement of a socially unacceptable goal by an acceptable one – or the value associated with it by 'denying the wish' ('I didn't really want it anyway') or repressing it. One may, finally, change the result. The realistic defence against anxiety is to try harder and therefore succeed, but the result may also be changed by selective reperception or misperception of the evidence. In an experiment by Wener and Rehm (1975) in which success-rate in a word association task was manipulated to be either 20 per cent or 80 per cent, nearly a third of the subjects *perceived* it to be somewhere around 50 per cent (a fact which receives surprisingly little comment from the paper's authors). A more complicated and by no means pathological variant is practised routinely between happily married couples: spouses maintain a highly idealized image of each other as compared with relevant others by a pattern of a biased causal attribution and wilful overlooking of evidence (Berger and Kellner, 1964; Hall and Taylor, 1976).

If all other defences have been attempted and have failed, what is left is revision of the expectancy, and if this expectancy is of a high order the results for the subject can be catastrophic. Depression, in this account, is interpreted as the subjective experience of being forced to revise one's expectancies about the most central and important areas of personal competence and ability to succeed. As such it may be seen as a basic element in many otherwise diverse pathological conditions; Seligman (1975, p. 76) describes it as 'the common cold of psychopathology'. In the best-known paradigm, reactive depression following sudden bereavement, the subject suddenly ceases to receive reinforcement of his picture of himself as lovable and admirable – he ceases to be loved and admired – because the source of the reinforcement has died.

To summarize, then, the synthesis of theories presented in this section represents anxiety and depression as essentially the outcome of cognitive states. Man defines himself in relation to the world by a set of expectancies as to what he can or cannot do and what he is free to do, and these are hierarchically ordered: underlying the expectation of a particular freedom or competence is a set of progressively more general constructs leading up to a core model of what one should be able to do in the world. Anxiety is generated when this core construct is questioned by the results of behaviour, and in general anxiety motivates the individual to try again or to take some other action which will reassert control, but if this is impracticable or unsuccessful it may lead to a redefinition or reperception of the world which will eliminate the discrepancy between expectation and result. Most cases of 'clinical depression' will exhibit considerable anxiety, but the end-state of the depressive process is a shattered self-image which leaves the person quite unable to orient himself in the world or predict positive consequences for his actions – he will expect only failure.

In the institutional setting we should expect that newly-received inmates – particularly those not yet familiar with the institution – should exhibit very considerable anxiety as they attempt to reassert their image of themselves in an environment which puts this image under severe threat. Gradually, however, the long-stay inmate – and particularly those whose term is an indeterminate one – will come to doubt their own competence in the face of an almost complete absence of the opportunity for control and they should lapse into depression, apathy and dependence.

A final point concerns the awareness of expectancy. Here we can only speculate. There is no necessity for expectancies to be constantly in consciousness. Indeed, while everything is going well one would expect them not to be present in consciousness: when riding a bicycle one does not constantly think to oneself, 'I am able to ride this bicycle'; one just rides it, generally thinking of something else or of nothing in particular. Only two sets of circumstances are liable to call expectancies to consciousness:

1. When comething has happened to cast doubt on them.
   OR
2. When they are mentioned specifically or attention is drawn to them.

The second may be a fault in a number of experiments on learning in humans; in 'manipulating expectancies' the experimenter may in fact be summoning up a higher order expectancy.

The synthesis of theories proposed above was developed in the mid-1970s as the basis for the empirical study reported here. It was developed out of necessity, to overcome problems with learned helplessness theory as it then stood. There was no explanation within the original theory for why learned helplessness affected some people and not others, and no entirely adequate account of why not *every* experience of uncontrolled aversive circumstances produced learned helplessness. Some concept of differential values and differential vulnerability was necessary for there to be an adequate explanation of the differential effects of institutions on their inmates. For completeness' sake, however, we should note that learned helplessness theory has not stood still since the mid-1970s and several new interpretations have been proposed which cover much of the same ground as the synthesis advanced here.

For instance, one important contribution is Susan Roth's 1980 paper stressing the importance of the *perception* of non-contingency, the prior expectancy of the subject, the amount of 'helplessness training', the attribution of causality made by the subject and the importance of the failure to control (including the degree to which it generalizes across different tasks rather than remaining task-specific). Her conclusion in general is that:

. . . people will be more likely to act on their environment (rather

than exhibit 'helplessness effects') the higher the value of potential reward and the higher the perceived probability of attaining
it. The value of future reward will be greater the more
psychologically threatening the failure or loss of control ... The
perceived probability of future reward will be lower the more
similar the subsequent situation *and the more general the attributions*
of causality made in response to the perceived non contingency.
Performance deficits or enhanced performance (reactance) will
result from the perception of non-contingency depending on the
nature of this double-edged effect . . .   (1980, p. 115, my
emphasis)

In the terms of the synthesis I have advanced above, one would
note that higher-order expectancies will contribute to those
associated with lower-order tasks. The expectancy associated
with a specific goal will in part be a function of expectancies
associated with goals of a higher order, to which the specific
goal is perceived by the subject as subordinate.

A more thoroughgoing reformulation, again in terms of
attributions of causality, has been presented by Abramson *et al*
(1978a, 1980). In this new formulation the important distinction is made between 'universal lack of control' and 'personal
lack of control' – between failing at a task which one believes is
soluble by comparable others but not by oneself and inability to
succeed where no one succeeds. The latter situation clearly has
no implications for any other situation, but the former implies
personal inadequacy and should produce less adequate and
motivated performance in other tasks. Distinctions are also
made between stable and unstable attributions of personal
helplessness ('I am stupid' versus 'I was exhausted') and global
versus specific attributions ('I am stupid' versus 'I am not good
at examinations'). In other words, the theory assumes a
hierarchy of importance to the negative statements which one
may be forced into believing about oneself, a conclusion
resembling that of the synthesis presented above. (For accounts
of clinical depression in this formulation, as a persistent
tendency to blame aversive experience on one's own incompetence, see Abramson *et al*, 1978b; Raps *et al*, 1982.)

A similar account has been developed (Bandura, 1977; Saltzer, 1982) from a rather different starting point. Bandura's 1977
paper suggested that human learning could be better explained
by positing an important central process which acted to unify
behaviour and give it overall long-term direction; he coined the
self-explanatory term 'self-efficacy' for this process. Saltzer

elaborates the concept to show that it has several components: belief in (expectation of) self-efficacy; belief in the likely outcome of one's behaviour; and the value of outcomes. Saltzer's paper works through these aspects to produce a model of reaction to circumstances not dissimilar to reformulated learned helplessness theory or the synthesis proposed here.

3.2:   *The design of the project*

In 1975 I carried out the fieldwork for an empirical study of life-sentence prisoners to test for deterioration as a result both of time in prison and of indeterminacy of sentence (the two are confounded in the design) and to illustrate how the theory of reaction to uncontrollable circumstances (which was outlined above) operates in the prison setting.

The study was envisaged as exploratory, and every effort was made to cover every aspect of the attitudinal/motivational background to abilities, insofar as was practicable within a prison setting. Thus a small sample researched in some depth was preferred to more superficial coverage of more substantial numbers, and rigour and precision of measurement have sometimes been sacrificed for the sake of covering all aspects. Extended and comparatively unstructured interviews were conducted, to give the subjects a chance to express their own feelings about the sentence and to let them direct the investigation into areas which might not have occurred to the investigator. A battery of formal tests was used, but this had to be kept short and interesting to retain the cooperation of the subjects. The prison files were used to build up a second-hand but detailed account of how the subjects had changed during the sentence, year by year.

It was decided to confine the study in the first instance to men convicted of a crime of homicide and serving life imprisonment. Both *Psychological Survival* and the Durham University study suffer from the weakness of tending to treat determinate and indeterminate sentences as though they were equivalent. It is true that the men serving them may in fact serve similar periods but in many other ways they are utterly different. In particular, the 'ground rules' are not the same for the two kinds of prisoner; even if the fixed-term fails parole, he still knows when he will be released, while the lifer, though he may know the average sentence, can never count on release until it is actually granted him. This uncertainty weighs heavily on lifers, for in some senses the whole of their future lives are at risk from moment to moment; they can never know whether they have condemned themselves to a vastly extended term in prison because of one momentary aberration.

> If you get into a fight with a fixed-termer you go up before the Governor and you both get the same punishment. But it goes on your record and when they are considering your release they see that there is violence on your record . . . (Life sentence prisoner, in a pilot interview)

One should note also that determinate-sentence men serving sentences comparable in length with the life sentence are fairly rare. The 'average' lifer serves between nine and twelve years, but terms of fifteen or sixteen years before release on licence are by no means uncommon and some men serve much longer.

All subjects came from one large maximum-security prison, nearly half of whose population are serving life sentences. Men who were younger than seventeen or older than forty-nine at conviction have been excluded; it is generally felt that young prisoners whose adolescence is spent in prison and men who have only a pension to go out to have problems untypical of life-sentence prisoners as a whole. Prisoners born outside the British Isles were also excluded, because some of the tests which have been used are culturally biased or at least require English as a first language.

The samples consist of men from three key points in the sentence: a 'reception' group of newly-received men, a 'middle' group of men in about their sixth year who had not yet been interviewed by the local review committee prior to their first review for possible release, and a 'hard core' group of men who had passed the 'average' release point and thus have to face the possibility of serving a very long term indeed. Fifteen men who had served more than eleven years were originally selected for this last group, but five had to be discarded during the course of the project because they either received a release date or were moved to a prison which suggested that release would not be long delayed. The ten men who were left had served an average of fourteen years by the time they were interviewed. The two other stages of sentence were represented by the twenty men in the prison's population who were in or near their sixth year (they had served an average of six years and five months by the time of interview) and the twenty most recently received men who were in the prison on 19 May 1975, when the sample was drawn, and who had served an average of nine months by the time of interview. As no special selection was exercised by the researcher, except to ensure that the subjects had served the relevant term, these three groups together are referred to as the 'random' sample below.

These groups are not necessarily entirely comparable with each other because of various selection effects built into the prison system. The prison concerned is an allocation centre for lifers, so that the 'reception' group is probably a more or less random cross-section of new lifers. It is also a maximum-security establishment, however, and has excellent educational facilities up to Open University level (but less extensive facilities for trade training) and full-time medical staff, so that the men there later in sentence will have been allocated on the basis of need rather than at random. 'Selection' effects are also inherent in length of sentence: release is a selective process, with men whose cases involved an element of sex or who have been noted as mentally abnormal (particularly psychopathic) tending to serve longer than the rest; also a small but not trivial proportion of lifers go to mental hospital under Section 72 of the Mental Health Act 1959, generally in the first two years of sentence, and a considerably smaller proportion come back later under Section 75. Thus there is a good reason to suppose that the men in prison who have served several years will differ from a random sample of newly-received men in important respects.

To eliminate some of this artificial variation, an attempt was made to build another kind of sample by matching 'hard core' men with men in the short-term groups – or with other suitable lifers in the prison who had served as near as possible to the right length of time, if suitable cases could not be found within the groups already formed. Three variables were used in the matching: age at conviction, victim-type (particularly whether the case involved sex or not) and the reports of doctors at trial or reception (particularly whether psycopathy was mentioned or not). The matching was by no means perfect even on these few variables, because the pool of available subjects of the relevant ages and victim-types was fairly small. The variance in victim-type and mental state is cut down considerably, however, and the matched groups are much more alike than the random ones in their distribution on all three variables combined. The matched 'middle' group had served an average of six years at the time of the interview and the 'reception' group about fifteen months.

Thus a total of sixty cases were finally selected. The 'random' and 'matched' samples are described above: the 'random' one consists of the ten hard-core men plus twenty men in each of the other two sentence-bands, and the 'matched' one of the same long termers plus ten men in each other sentence-band; four of the 'reception' matched group and six of the 'middle' one also appear in the corresponding random group. (When examining the interrelation of characteristics, the 'total' sample consisting quite simply of all sixty cases will often be used, to give a larger sample size.) Numbers in each group and the extent of overlap are shown in Table 1.

TABLE 1: *Samples used in the lifer project*

Sample:	'Random'	'Matched'	Cases occurring in both	Total
Group:				
'Hard-core'	10	10	10	10
'Middle'	20	10	6	24
'Reception'	20	10	4	26
Total	50	30	20	60

Data collection was in three parts: a battery of formal tests, a relatively unstructured interview and a search of prison files (including medical case-papers) for relevant information recorded by prison staff and visiting psychiatrists, social workers etc. Interviews with the prisoners, excluding the formal tests, lasted on average for about an hour and a half, though surprisingly the interviewer was invited back to continue the discussion on another occasion by about one man in four. The interviews were of course voluntary, and several men refused at the first application. Most later relented but four men were not seen at all (all, unfortunately, 'hard-core' men), so that only file data are available for these, and one man refused the formal tests although he was willing to be interviewed. Every prisoner was promised confidentiality at the start of the interview but warned that the researcher had no power of interference in individual cases, whether for good or ill, and that although he was employed by the Home Office he had no influence on release or prison movement and could not act as a channel for the resolution of individual grievances. He also spent a few minutes explaining the role of the Home Office Research Unit (his employers) and of psychological 'tests' used as a means of characterizing *groups*, to allay anxieties that the research might be some kind of surreptitious psychological assessment carried out on behalf of the 'system'. The prisoners appeared to believe what was said to them, but of course one cannot be sure of that. The formal 'tests', which took about an hour to administer in total, were split into three batteries and used at designated points as an opportunity to change the topic of conversation and to vary the pace of the interview.

Adding a crude psychiatric classification to the variables discussed earlier as characterizing learned helplessness and the view of deterioration common in prisoners gave a list of twelve areas for examination:

1. depression and hopelessness;
2. anxiety;
3. introversion;
4. neuroticism and emotionality;
5. apathy;
6. dependence on staff and routine;
7. motivation to do one's best;
8. sociability;
9. interest in the outside world and outside contacts;
10. concern with release;
11. 'orientation' in time and length of future time perspective;
12. general psychiatric state.

These are mostly imprecise concepts of considerable generality and they have been operationalized in a variety of ways. For some aspects of them, 'paper and pencil' tests exist or could be devised without making too many assumptions. For some there were fairly obvious 'hard' data available: number of letters, for example, measures one aspect of interest in the outside world. For most, assessment had to be made on the basis of what the man said in the interview or what was said about him in the files. The information on which these assessments were made tends of course to be incomplete and liable to bias. Wherever possible, therefore, more than one measure of each concept was taken from each source, to increase the chances of covering all aspects of the concept, and in all except 'medical assessment' more than one source has been used in an attempt to increase the validity of the measurement.

The principal psychometric instruments used were the Cornell Medical Index, Beck's Hopelessness Scale and a shortened version of the Minnesota Multiphasic Personality Inventory (MMPI). The MMPI (Hathaway and McKinley, 1940, describe its construction) is a list of statements about themselves and the work with which subjects are invited to agree or disagree; the items were picked to discriminate between differently diagnosed groups of mental patients and between mental patients and 'normals' without this purpose becoming too obvious to the patients themselves. A large number of different diagnostic scales have been 'discovered' in the course of the test's use but the validity of many of them is seriously in question. Six scales were scored in the current research which appear to be validly interpretable:

1. Hs (Hypocondriasis), constructed by McKinley and Hathaway (1940), which has been shown by factor analysis to have a large and reliable principal factor of 'health concern' (Comrey, 1957a);

2. D (Depression), constructed by Hathaway and McKinley (1942) to distinguish clinically depressed subjects from normals and shown by factor analysis to have quite reasonable construct validity (Comrey, 1957b);

3. Pt (Psychaesthenia), first reported by McKinley and Hathaway (1942), a scale with a very strong loading on general neurosis or emotionality (Comrey, 1958);

4. ES (Ego-strength), a scale which is said to show a relationship to success in therapy (Barron, 1953; Taft, 1957; Gottesman, 1959);

5. MA (Manifest Anxiety), a scale which Janet Taylor (1953) constructed by asking practising psychoanalysts to pick test items most indicative of a current state of excessive anxiety, but which despite its name appears rather to measure the *trait* of being susceptible to behavioural disruption during times of stress (Eriksen and Davids, 1955; Siegman, 1956; Stanton, 1971);

6. Si (Social Introversion), a straightforward introversion/

extraversion scale constructed and validated against other accepted measures of this trait (Drake, 1946; Drake and Thiede, 1948).

(The entire MMPI has more than five hundred items, which seemed an unreasonable volume with which to face a prisoner, but a cut-down version of one hundred and sixty-eight items appears to work almost as well, and this is what was used here – see Overall *et al*, 1973; Overall and Gomez-Mont, 1974.) The Hopelessness Scale (Beck *et al*, 1974) is a quick measure of pessimistic future perspective and the Cornell Medical Index a list of physical and mental 'symptoms' for the subject to check which was designed for preliminary medical screening but has proved to relate well to neuroticism in the general population (Broadman *et al*, 1949, 1952; Culpan *et al*, 1960; Zakia, 1969).

Some of the variables which these 'questionnaire' scales did not attack were tapped using a semi-projective instrument designed by Penelope Dixon (1967), in which subjects are presented with pairs of photographs of the same number and sex/age of people and asked during a fixed time to list any differences they might notice between the pictures in each pair. Dixon used this as a test of affective flatness – the tendency not to impute emotion to others – and found marked differences in this respect between depressives and normals, and this variable was scored for the current research. (The most extreme response of this kind which I came across was that of one man who said of two pictures of young girls 'The mouth is curved up in one picture and down in the other', avoiding any reference to girls smiling; on the other hand, one man's responses were difficult to interpret because he was a keen amateur photographer and spent more time commenting on the quality of the reproduction than on the people in the photographs.)

Finally, tests were specially constructed of Apathy, Sociability, Outside Interest, Motivation, Competition and Dependence on Staff/Routine. These involved prisoners sorting sets of statements into rank order on the criteria 'Things which are important to the prisoner', 'Things which help me to get through sentence' and 'Things I most like doing in association time'. These tests were a mistake, from the point of view of research design. They were of high 'face validity' – they were constructed from material gathered in pilot interviews as a list of activities or attitudes 'obviously' bearing on the variables to be measured – but there was no formal examination of validity

or reliability. This means that if they had produced results
different from those of the other 'paper and pencil' tests there
would have been no way of telling whether the differences were
due to the traits measured or to unreliability or invalidity of the
measuring-instruments. The fault does not matter, as it happens, because their results are completely in line with those of
other tests. (What was *not* a mistake was to ask subjects *why* they
put ranked statements high or low; this yielded useful information used to advantage below.)

I made 'ratings' from the interview material of a number of
the concepts and also made some ratings of the prisoner and his
behaviour during the interview. The prison's central files, the
files held in the prison wing and the case-papers in the prison
hospital were examined for reports of the man's mental state,
attitudes, work performance, spare-time activities, and in
general his 'progress' year by year since reception. From the
records for the last two years several ratings of attitudes were
made and have been used below. In addition a record was made
of the number of 'applications' – requests made of staff, ranging
from trivial administrative matters to complaints and petitions
– of punishments received and of visits to the prison hospital
during the last year and of the number of letters sent and
received (and visits) during a given three-month period of each
year. The files also yielded a fair amount of demographic and
descriptive information, supplemented as necessary from the
HORU 'Lifer Index'.

The analysis of these data proceeds in two parts. Information
about current state – the psychological tests, and ratings based
on interviews and files which refer to what is currently thought
to be true of the prisoner – forms the basis of a cross-sectional
analysis. This information was readily quantifiable and has
been analysed chiefly by means of correlation and partial correlation. Secondly, 'longitudinal' information was derived from
the files and the interview proposals. This is much more
anecdotal in nature, much more nebulous and far less amenable
to quantitative analysis: different prisoners remembered different aspects of their past during the interview and staff report-
ing 'second hand' on different prisoners highlight different
aspects of prison life. Some of this material is summarized in
this chapter and more extended accounts are given later in the
book.

The total record contains a vast amount of data: nearly three
hundred items of information were discarded at the stage of

preliminary analysis because they related neither to time served nor to any interesting item of demographic or descriptive information. Because of this it was seen as essential that a technique of analysis be used which could represent complex interrelationships economically and be presented in the minimum amount of space. Correlation seemed the best choice and it was for this reason that all variables were reduced to three-point scales; although this results in a loss of information, it prevents distortion of the results by one or two extreme and untypical cases. Partial correlations have been used to search for spurious apparent relationships resulting from the correlation of demographic factors with time served. The drawbacks of a correlational approach, with sixty or fewer cases and only three-point scales, are evident: the technique lacks power, so that some weak but actually significant relationships may be missed, and the actual size of the correlation coefficients may be misleading (they are probably too low). However, constraints of space and the number of variables make the more powerful and precise techniques too cumbersome.

3.3:   'Cross-sectional' results

Table 2 gives results of the psychological tests for the 'reception' and 'mid-sentence' groups of lifers in the study. (The 'matched' sample did not differ much from the 'random' one – except in introversion, a point to which we shall return – so the two have been combined to give slightly larger numbers.) There would appear to be little of significance distinguishing the two groups. 'Reception' men are less introverted than men in the middle of sentence but have higher scores on the 'mental' subset of the Cornell Medical Index and Beck's Hopelessness Scale (the last-named difference being significant but not large). Overall there is a very slight but consistent tendency towards *higher* scores among newly-received men (except in the 'constructed' scales); however, the differences do not reach statistical significance. Table 3, giving ratings of psychological traits derived from files and interviews, shows a similar pattern; there is a consistent tendency for newly received men to be rated as more anxious, depressed or emotional but in no case does it reach significance.

The main conclusion has to be that there is precious little difference between the two samples in general emotional state.

TABLE 2: *Psychological test results for two groups of life-sentence prisoners*

Sentence-group			'Reception' (26)	'Mid-sentence' (24)	
CORNELL MEDICAL INDEX	Total score	Mean s.d.	32.40 21.66	29.7 22.06	
	'Mental' score	Mean s.d.	4.5 2.26	2.8 2.84	p<.05
MMPI	Hs	Mean s.d.	14.4 4.67	13.1 5.33	
	D	Mean s.d.	9.1 2.60	8.5 2.78	———
	Pt	Mean s.d.	5.4 3.01	4.9 2.69	
	Si	Mean s.d.	7.8 2.29	10.0 4.96	p.<.05
	Ego-strength scale	Mean s.d.	42.7 5.87	43.6 5.06	
	Manifest anxiety scale	Mean s.d.	20.2 8.18	17.3 7.61	
	Hopelessness scale	Mean s.d.	8.6 2.32	6.7 3.20	p<.05
	Flatness of affect scale	Mean s.d.	4.4 2.32	3.6 2.40	
CONSTRUCTED SCALES	Apathy	Mean s.d.	3.4 1.86	3.3 1.59	
	Sociability	Mean s.d.	3.5 1.78	3.9 1.94	
	Outside interest	Mean s.d.	5.0 1.52	4.3 1.21	
	Motivation	Mean s.d.	3.8 1.44	4.2 1.22	
	Competition	Mean s.d.	2.2 1.85	2.6 1.58	
	Dependence	Mean s.d.	3.9 1.69	4.2 1.40	

TABLE 3: *Ratings of psychological state for two groups of life-sentence prisoners*

		Sentence-group:	
		'Reception'	*'Mid-sentence'*
	N	26	24
ANXIETY			
Rating of medical comments:			
None		19	20
Mild		2 }7	2 }4
Strong		5	2
Ratings of comments by other staff:			
None		14	16
Mild		8 }12	6 }8
Strong		4	2
Ratings of interview protocol:			
Calm, unworried		2 }10	5 }15
Neither		8	10
Anxious		16	9
DEPRESSION			
Rating of medical comments:			
None		22	21
Mild		2 }4	2 }3
Strong		2	1
Ratings of comments by other staff:			
None		13	16
Mild		9 }13	7 }8
Strong		4	1
Rating of interview protocol:			
Cheerful		5	9
Neither		9	6
Depressed		12	9
NEUROTICISM/EMOTIONALITY			
Rating of medical comments:			
None		20	16
Mild		2 }6	7 }8
Strong		4	1
Rating of comments by other staff:			
None		22	20
Mild		? }4	3 }4
Strong		2	1
Interviewer's rating of amount of strong feeling displayed in interview:			
None		4	7
Some		9	8
Much		13	9

There are no signs of consistent growth in neuroticism/ emotionality, anxiety, depression, apathy, affective flatness or the range of variables supposedly connected with institutional- ization for which scales were specially constructed. The only test whose results show an increase with length of sentence is Drake's scale of Social Introversion, a finding which parallels a result of the Durham University research. Despite the predic- tions of the 'learned helplessness' model, the tests of depression, apathy, motivation and dependence on staff or routine do not show any marked loss of competence during the sentence. (Hopelessness, a crucial variable for this model, *decreases* significantly.) Indeed, in both Tables it is possible to detect a slight trend in the opposite direction to that predicted by the model. While most of the differences do not come anywhere near reaching statistical significance, the bulk of them are in the same direction, with subjects scoring consistently a little higher in the reception group than at mid sentence.

Overall one might be tempted to see the Tables as demon- strating two things: that such changes as there are may consist in recovery from initial shock rather than in effects of time spent in prison – though there are suggestions of increased with- drawal as sentence progresses – and that any such patterns tend to be swamped by the individual differences between subjects irrespective of time served. Examining the twelve 'areas of study' listed earlier in this chapter adds a few points of indi- vidual interest but does not change this overall picture. The forty-five variables included in the analysis are listed in Table 4, with their correlations with stage of sentence for the three 'samples'.

Interest in the Outside World   Despite the findings of mental hospital studies, the current study does not suggest that *interest* in the outside world declines as a function of time served in prison among the majority of life-sentence prisoners. None of the 'attitudinal' measures taken in interview – the INTEREST card-sort scale, whether the man expressed such interest during the interview itself and whether he mentioned his own outside contacts in his responses to the semi-projective Dixon picture- comparison task – correlates with time served at more than a chance level. *Actual* involvement in the outside world, as measured by number of visits or letters and by the ratio of letters received to letters sent, declines with sentence length (signifi- cantly so in the case of the former and nearly so in the latter).

TABLE 4: *Correlations of variables with time served in samples of life-sentence prisoners*

Variable	Sample: Total	Random	Matched
Formal tests:			
INTEREST scale	−.15	−.11	−.28
SOCIABILITY scale	.14	.11	.17
MOTIVATION scale	−.10	−.08	−.31
COMPETITION scale	.24	.25	.28
APATHY scale	.07	.14	.07
DEPENDENCY scale	.15	.13	.29
MMPI Si scale	.39*	.33[+]	.59**
Picture comparison task:			
Dixon score (comments have an affective component)	.29[+]	.45*	−.03
Outside contacts mentioned in the course of the task	−.01	−.08	−.07
Interview data:			
Interest in outside contacts	−.03	−.01	.06
Unsociable	.21	.21	.32
Attending classes is important	−.41*	−.46**	−.54**
Keeping fit is important	−.01	−.01	.28
Highly motivated	−.14	−.09	−.56*
On side of staff or benefits	.46**	.45*	.62**
Feels powerless about parole	.13	.18	.05
Release mentioned spontaneously	.05	.03	.08
Future time-perspective	−.41*	−.38*	−.43[+]
Lives in past, v future	.00	.13	−.19
Interviewer's ratings:			
Cell looked clean and tidy	−.13	−.10	−.21
Cell looked like home	.02	.04	.05
Subject seemed apathetic	.22	.22	.29
File ratings:			
Unsociable	−.01	.05	−.24
Apathetic	.25[+]	.28[+]	.30
Quiet, settled	.11	.17	.18
Institutionalised	.35*	.49**	.11
On side of staff, v prisoners	.14	.13	.16
Lives in past, v future	−.38*	−.38*	−.46[+]
Lives in present	.17	.25	.10
Medical assessments:			
Psychosis	.11	.09	.23
Personality disorder	−.19	−.12	−.34
Sexual abnormality	.23	.21	.15
Immaturity	.15	.19	.11
Other data:			
Number of letters or visits	−.34*	−.34*	−.33
Ratio of letters 'in' to 'out'	−.20	−.24	−.22
Discipline offences, refusing work	.00	.07	.00
Offences/complaints against staff	−.08	−.15	−.14
Hospital visits	.23	.16	.35
Applications	.11	.06	.10
Descriptive information:			
Age at interview	.38*	.48**	.27
Victim scale	.19	.26	.00
Crime involved sex	.14	.25	.00
Social contacts at reception	−.14	−.21	−.17
Previous convictions	−.05	−.01	−.16
Previous penal incarceration	.06	.10	.06

Looking at the actual numbers, in the 'random' sample the 'reception' men received or sent an average of thirty letters in three months, compared with about fourteen for the 'middle' group; for the hard core the average is about sixteen but with a very large variance – a few men sent and received many letters, but most very few. The 'reception' men received an average of 2.7 visits during the same period and the 'middle' group 2.2 – the difference is not significant – but the men in the hard core received only 1.4. The pattern in the 'matched' sample is similar: the decline in correspondence is less extreme – the 'reception' men sent and received fewer letters – but differences in visiting are more so. By and large, contact with 'natal' family (parents, siblings, children) was preserved; 70 per cent of the 'hard core' were still in contact at the end of their eleventh year, though in some cases the contact amounted only to an exchange of Christmas and birthday cards. Wives and girlfriends, on the other hand, had nearly all lost contact by the end of the fifth year, and most dropped off very early in sentence.

Other factors than time served are related to both actual involvement and interest in the outside world. Actual involvement shows a much higher correlation with the state of the man's social relationships when he was received on sentence, and expressed interest in the outside is weakly related to level of actual involvement. Controlling for time already served and initial social contacts by means of partial correlation does not change the relationship of the attitudinal variables to current rate of correspondence, and no combination of partialing significantly raises their correlation with time served or state of social contacts at reception. Actual level of correspondence remains related at a highly significant level with time served even when 'initial state of social contacts' has been controlled.

Even life-sentence prisoners seem to retain their *interest* in the outside world, and 40 per cent of them spontaneously mentioned in interview that visiting and correspondence arrangements needed improving (Lawton, 1978), a proportion similar to the one given by Newton *et al* (1972) for shorter-term men. Farber (1944) found that prisoners were most distressed about their outside contacts at the time when the relationship was beginning to decline and that they sometimes cut off contact themselves to finish the process quickly; cases of this are reported by Cohen and Taylor (1972). Among the lifers, however, there were no such instances, except that engaged men tended to offer their fiancées their freedom soon after conviction, an offer which was generally taken up after only a very brief struggle.

However, there were some slight indications that family contacts, often an overwhelmingly important consideration at the beginning of the sentence, may lose their primacy as a survival consideration in the mind of the man who has served several years. The lifer sample whom I interviewed were given three packs of statements to sort into order of frequency as a spare time activity, importance to the prisoner and usefulness as a way of 'getting through sentence' (the 'constructed scales'), and it proved illuminating to count the number of packs in which a statement referring to family contact was selected as first choice. Fifty per cent of the newly-received prisoners put 'family' cards top in two or three of the packs and only a quarter did not put them top in any. Only a fifth of the 'mid-sentence' men chose at least two (and none of the 'hard core') and half chose none. The trend by offence-type is equally marked, suggesting perhaps that the effect stems from the family rather than the prisoner: only 11 per cent of the 'sex offenders' chose 'family' cards more than once and nearly 60 per cent chose none, compared with 43 per cent and around a third in the other offence categories. (There was a slight trend with age, but this probably relates to offence-type, as the 'sex offenders' tend to be rather older on average than other murderers. Experience of previous imprisonment did not appear to have any effect at all.)

Sociability and Interest in People   Six variables were considered as possible measures of sociability and interest in people:

1. The Si scale from the MMPI;
2. the constructed SOCIABILITY scale;
3. Dixon's measure of emotional responsiveness;
4. whether the man was described as unsociable by himself in interview; OR
5. by the staff in the files; AND
6. his level of correspondence.

They did not relate strongly to each other and there was no evidence of a general trait: the only interesting relationships were weak ones between interview rating of unsociability and level of correspondence and between social introversion (MMPI scale) and flatness of affect (Dixon score). The only variable (apart from level of correspondence, which was discussed above) bearing a strong relationship to time served is the

MMPI measure of social introversion, a scale designed to assess the extent of the subject's interest in social and outgoing activities; controlling for level of correspondence leaves its significance unchanged.

The increase in social introversion as sentence progresses is likely to be an effect of the men's attitude to prison and to the sentence rather than a selection effect: controlling for age and victim-type does not reduce the correlation. In the matched sample the trait is weakly related to work record before reception (which might be taken as a reflection of general lifestyle) and to the reception diagnosis of sexual abnormality. In both samples there is also a weak but statistically significant relationship with the time men thought they had left before release, and none of the men who expected to serve at least another ten years scored low on the Si scale. When all these factors are taken into account, however, the correlation between Si and time served remains significant. The fact that the relationship is stronger in the matched sample than the random one, however, hints at interaction effects: some kinds of people may be more prone than others to show increased introversion as sentence progresses.

The finding that introversion increases with time spent inside, which was also a finding of the Durham University work (see Heskin *et al*, 1973), is an important one for one theory of how people come to be 'criminals'. Eysenck's elaborate synthesis of a personality theory and a learning-theory account of how 'conscience' is acquired depends for part of its force on the 'finding' that people who score high on extraversion and neuroticism are over-represented in prison and other 'deviant' populations. It now appears, however, that extraversion is not a stable trait but decreases with time spent in prison – at least for men serving substantial sentences. Moreover, shorter-term prisoners often do not exhibit high extraversion, though they do tend to score highly on the neuroticism scale (Fitch, 1962; Black and Gregson, 1973; Crookes, 1979). Extraversion does not, indeed, appear at all as a crucial descriptive variable of prisoners' personalities in factor analytic studies (Heskin *et al*, 1977). As Crookes comments on such findings:

> Unfortunately the high E, with its relationship to poor conditionability, low 'arousal' and sensation-seeking, is the most important part of (Eysenck's) theory as an explanation for delinquent behaviour; the high N seems to be regarded simply as a factor which intensifies behaviour of any kind.

The Si scale may not, of course, be a true measure of introversion among prisoners, as it contains questions about behaviours no longer available to the subject, such as 'going to parties'. To some extent this problem was circumvented by rephrasing the questions so that they referred to pre-prison behaviour – 'When you *used to* go to parties, did you . . .?' – but an element of doubt must still remain, as the pre-prison period is further in the past for a man who has been inside for several years than for one who has only recently been received. (One should note that this objection holds also for Eysenck's use of similar scales.)

Apathy and Motivation   Under the headings of apathy and lessened motivation twelve variables were considered: scores on the constructed scales of (1) MOTIVATION to improve or do one's best, (2) COMPETITION and (3) APATHY; whether the man said in interview that (4) attending classes and keeping the mind active or (5) remaining physically fit, was important; (6) whether he described himself in interview as highly motivated or as wanting to do things which implied high motivation; (7) whether he seemed to the interviewer to be apathetic in his manner; (8) the state of his cell; whether he was described in the files as (9) of low motivation and apathetic, or as (10) quiet, settled and a 'good prisoner'; (11) whether he had often been reported for refusing work; and (12) whether more letters came in than he sent out. Again there is little intercorrelation, except that scores on the MOTIVATION scale, describing oneself as highly motivated and considering it important to keep one's mind active, tend to go together. Otherwise there is no evidence of a general trait.

Two of these variables are significantly related to time served. First, the man's belief that it is important to attend classes and keep one's mind active tends to diminish with time served. The effect seems entirely due to the small number of 'hard-core' men who felt this, which is not remarkable. The second variable, staff rating of apathy, has only a weak relationship with time served which again is apparently due to the scores from the hard-core group.

Dependency   Another twelve variables were taken to measure aspects of dependency, routine, orientation towards prison staff and 'institutionalization' in general. These were: (1) a card-sort scale of DEPENDENCY on routine and orientation towards staff; (2) whether the man described himself in interview as being on the side of the staff or as benefiting from his contact with some member of staff; (3) whether he complained of his powerlessness in the face of the parole system; (4) whether he mentioned release spontaneously; (5) whether his cell was clean or dirty (the interviews were mostly conducted in the men's cells), and (6) whether it showed signs of being regarded as his 'home'; whether he was described in the files (7) as institutionalized, or (8) as quiet and well settled, and (9) as on the side of the staff; (10) the number of discipline offences (or complaints) against staff in the last year; (11) the number of visits to the prison hospital in the last year; and (12), the number of 'applications' made. (The last two were seen as rough measures of the amount of actual contact with staff.) Only two increased significantly with time served: self-description as on the staff side or benefiting from contact with them, and file description as institutionalized.

The self-description clusters to some extent with other measures of 'being on the staff side' – staff ratings of the man as 'on the side of staff', or as 'quiet and well settled', and low incidence of offences or complaints against staff – but these do not themselves correlate significantly with time served. The increase with time served is observable in both the random and the matched samples (it is greater in the latter). In the random sample this variable correlates with being in the 'sex' victim-type, but controlling for the effect of this does not materially diminish the relationship of the former with time served. The relationship is not a linear one, however. Between the 'reception' and 'middle' groups there is some increase, but not enough to raise the correlation to significance. This is probably to be seen, therefore, as a property of the 'hard core', a change of attitude perhaps which occurs when the man realizes that he has passed the 'average' date of release and is likely to be inside for a very long time.

The findings concerning staff descriptions of 'institutionalization' are more difficult to interpret. This variable, which shows a marked relationship with time served in the random sample, is barely correlated at all with time served in the matched sample (see Table 4). In itself this would suggest a 'selection effect' – people likely to be called institutionalized could be drafted selectively into the prison because of some aspect of the regime or the medical facilities, for example – and the suggestion is reinforced when we find that it also correlates with victim-type and with initial state of social contacts. However, controlling for these variables in the total samples hardly reduces at all the correlation with time served. A more plausible explanation would seem to be that while there may be certain types of lifer who are likely to be (or to be called) institutionalized almost irrespective of how long they have served, among the remainder the term spent inside does seem to have some effect on the use of the term. In the absence of systematic correlation with other indicators, however, we cannot necessarily take the description at face value.

Time Perspective   Four measures of time perspective and temporal orientation were considered: in interview, the span from the present to the furthest future time mentioned (before the question of release was raised by the interviewer), and whether the subject talked more about the past or the future; from the files, whether the subject was described as being more concerned with the past or the future, and whether he appeared to live more in the present than in either. The observed constriction of future time span as sentence progresses is best interpreted not as evidence of a change in attitude, but rather as an artefact of the structure of the sentence; men early in sentences see a long time stretching ahead of them; many men at seven years see themselves getting out within one or two reviews (i.e., within two to four years); the hard-core men see only as far as the next review (one to two years). Very few men spoke spontaneously of what they would do after release and those who did seemed to 'see' only a little way into their future lives. 'Barrier effects' of this kind, where a major landmark in the future constricts future time perspective, have been noted previously in a number of contexts; Lessing (1968), for example, found a shrinkage of future time perspective as school children came nearer to the date of leaving school and Landau (1969) reports a similar result with fixed-term prisoners and date of release. The tendency to look forward only as far as release date may be seen as 'living in the present', but the file data would not seem to bear this out. Some of the hard-core men were described as concerned only with day-to-day existence and some of the newly-received men appeared to be making grandiose plans for self-education, but this does not greatly affect the overall picture.

The interview rating of 'living in the past' does not correlate with time served. Although the offence and the man's life before reception were deliberately not made a subject of enquiry – so many of the people who interview lifers are primarily concerned with the offence – a surprisingly large number of men wanted to talk about them. It is probable, therefore, that the staff rating of the amount men 'dwell in the past' is the more useful measure, being formed over a period of time rather than in one rather artificial situation. It shows a negative relationship with time served, more pronounced in the matched sample than the random one but otherwise not much affected by demographic and historical differences.

Psychiatric State Current medical descriptions of tendency towards psychosis, personality disorders, sexual abnormality or immaturity were recorded from hospital case-papers and medical reports to various official bodies. None of them showed any association with time served.

Summarizing the results spelled out in the last few pages, there was no increase with time served in tendency towards psychosis, personality disorders, sexual abnormality or immaturity of thinking and no loss of interest in the outside world – though perhaps the outside becomes less desperately important as time passes. Four minor differences appeared to be associated with time served: longer-serving men had a reduced future time perspective (the future events mentioned in interview were not so distant from the present), a fact undoubtedly related to the timing of reviews for release; they appeared to have a greater tendency to talk about the past rather than the future, as assessed from staff reports (though this was not apparent in interview); they were more likely to be labelled 'institutionalized' by staff; and they became increasingly introverted as sentence progressed. Two changes appeared related not to time served as such but to membership of the 'hard core' of men beyond the average release date: keeping the mind active by attending classes ceased to be seen as important and the men came to see their attitudes as increasingly aligned with those of the staff (though this did not seem to be reflected in the staff's view of the prisoner). There was no evidence of apathy about release even after being turned down repeatedly, such as might be predicted by the 'learned helplessness' model, and no evidence whatsoever for a general syndrome of 'institutionalization' or 'deterioration'.

At the end of the interview subjects were asked: 'Given that you have to do your sentence, what would you change about the system or the prison?' – a very good question, suggested to me by the first lifer I interviewed, which generally elicited quite a list of complaints and grievances over the way things are run, together often with well-informed and constructive suggestions for improvement. A content analysis of these responses published by Lawton (1977) reinforces the contention that institutionalization is not common in prison. Far from becoming preoccupied with trivial details, men who had served considerable terms were most likely to express concern about broad issues of communication and maintenance of self-respect within the prison system, the general organization of prison labour and the opportunities available for maintaining one's familiarity with the real outside world. It was the newly-received men, particularly those with little or no previous experience of prison, who were most concerned with the details of day-to-day regime.

3.4:   *'Longitudinal' results*

The model tested in the previous section, based on studies in the 'learned helplessness' genre, hypothesized that the effects of total institutions would be emotional disturbance and reaction in the early months after reception, consequent on disruption of lifestyle, followed by rational adaptation to the demands of the institution. This would be followed, in its turn, by depression, apathy, unsociability, loss of interest in the outside world, lessened capacity to deal with novel problems, increased dependence on routine and the support of the staff – in other words some or all of the phenomena of learned helplessness or institutionalism, terms which were seen as equivalent in meaning.

   To some extent the model is accurate in its predictions. The descriptions of how the lifers in this survey spoke and behaved when they were first received show that when people come in at the start of their sentence, particularly when it is for the first time, the shock is very great. Suddenly they have lost the whole pattern of their lives and the whole of the reinforcement to which they are accustomed. About three-quarters of the total lifer sample – forty-six out of sixty men – received medical reports at reception which suggested some degree of psychological disturbance, though not necessarily amounting to a treatable mental abnormality. Thirty per cent were described as showing considerable anxiety (evenly divided in its manifestation between men who were timid and withdrawn and men who showed a high degree of emotionality and intropunitive hostility). Eight men (13 per cent) were described as depressed, another nine (15 per cent) alternated between anxiety and depression, and three appeared to be in shock. A sixth of the sample showed emotionality amounting to belligerence: they were aggressive, hostile, tense and prone to outbursts of temper. For fourteen men there were no particular medical comments, but staff reports or their own memories elicited in interview suggested that ten of them showed one or another of these reactions.

With only four exceptions – men who were sustained by outside contacts, or already familiar with total institutions or deprived lifestyles, or not yet considering the sentence as inevitable – all of the lifers in the sample showed considerable emotional disturbance during the year or so following their reception into prison. From other reports, such a pattern would appear fairly typical for reception into any kind of total institution. This dies down in most people, however, as they settle into the new life. People adapt to even the most extraordinary privations: even concentration camps are situations which have rules and these become to some extent predictable after a while; it is possible, to some extent, to survive under them.

Beyond the point of adapting to the initial shock the simple picture of 'effects of sentence' breaks down. It does not necessarily become wrong – the *pressure* towards constriction of life and child-like behaviour, towards dependence on routine, towards depression, apathy and 'giving up the struggle', are very evident when one talks to people in institutions or looks at the lives that they lead. To suppose that such pressures must always have effects, however, is to leave the person out of the equation. What one sees in long-term prisoners, or people who have spent long terms in orphanages or hospitals, is partly explicable in terms of institutional pressure towards conformity and dependence, just as civil servants experience a pressure towards rigidity of thought and teachers and lawyers towards pomposity of expression. In institutions, the way that people are coping after they have been inside for eight or ten years is partly to be explained by the institution, but only indirectly.

Looking at case histories in retrospect, what one does tend to find is that the initial period of shock, anxiety and 'floundering around' is very much a search for a role, a period of experimentation in which a variety of styles are tried out until the subject finds one that he can maintain. (To some extent this may be an unconscious process, but to some extent it is deliberate and thought out; long-term prisoners do not lack advice from other prisoners and from staff about how they should 'do their time' and many of the lifers I talked to spoke about sitting down and working out how to survive.) The process can be seen to some extent as one of learning to give up one's previous life and adapt to the new one. For example, during the interview when subjects were asked to put sixteen activities in order of importance to prisoners a variety of items were selected by different people as the most important – the most common were 'keeping his nose clean' and 'staying in touch with his family' – with no obvious effect of time served on the choice made. When one considers the *reasons* given for the choice, however, a clearer pattern emerges. A third of each sample nominated some activity as the most important merely because it was pleasurable or helped to pass the time. A third of the total sample gave a reason which involved either proving fitness for release or improving one's capabilities for the sake of the improvement – in other words, an activity and goal appropriate to prison – while the remaining third said something involving the retention of past lifestyle and mentality – staying fit, not allowing oneself to deteriorate in prison, making sure one still has a family to go to on release, continuing to understand what is happening in the outside world. 'Prison activity' answers were twice as common among men who had already served a substantial part of the sentence as among men still in their first two years, and the reverse is true of answers which involved retention of the past.

The main outcome of the longitudinal analysis is that prisoners did not deteriorate, because they found ways of coming to terms with the prison environment and using it for their own purposes. Three men in the 'hard-core' category did appear to have deteriorated more or less completely, but all effectively 'broke down' soon after reception and all had failed to cope effectively with the world outside as well. Most men, however, managed to assert some measure of control over their prison experience and a few managed effectively to 'negate' or 'escape from' it by forcing a redefinition of circumstances such that prison was an inconvenience rather than an environment exerting total control, or even became a facilitating environment. (For the most extreme and bizarre example of such 'redefinition' see the case of Edward Guildford, discussed in the next chapter.) In general prisoners were able somehow to find a *modus vivendi* in prison.

3.5: *Interim conclusions: a 'reactance' explanation*

It would appear from these results that learned helplessness does not account for institutionalization among life-sentence prisoners because little or no institutionalization occurs. However, in my first substantial account of this work (Sapsford, 1979a) I was able to construct an explanation which remained consonant with the theories outlined at the beginning of this chapter given two points which are crucial to the argument:

1. The finding that the 'learned helplessness' paradigm does not appear to predict successfully the effects of prison on the prisoner is a finding specific to prisons. Reports on concentration camps suggest that apathy, hopelessness and general 'giving up' may be common in institutions where the conditions of life are more repressive than in prisons. Studies of mental hospitals also generally show a far higher incidence of 'institutionalization' than has been revealed in a majority of the prison studies.

2. The prisoner is aware of the pressures towards 'institutionalization' to which he is subject and his feeling about them is often intense and vehement.

That very strong pressures towards institutionalization exist in prison will not be doubted by anyone who has spent time in and around prisons and that prisoners and staff are both acutely aware of these pressures is equally apparent.

> The thing about prison is the lack of *need* to do things and make decisions by yourself. (But others still *want* to use their minds and go in for other things like education, or painting.) The routine is insidious. Men go the same way to work, from the same landing, down the same stairs, through the same door, day after day. If they've got to go out of a different door one day – the other one's being painted, say – it's as though the world had fallen about their ears. In the old exercise yards, where the men are walking round in a circle, if you yelled 'about turn', they'd be utterly confused. They like to know what's what and to have things stay that way. (Partly our fault – it suits us to have things like that.) I suppose we teach them to conform and to obey

orders. You have to. If there's a fire, you cannot explain to each man separately why he has to leave the building.

This description of the pressures exerted by prison routine, given me by an officer in a prison hostel, agrees very well with the picture of prison held by many life-sentence prisoners. Asked 'What is the sentence like for people who serve *very* long terms?', about a third of the total sample did not mention any particular pressures, but another third thought that such men ran the *risk* of slowing mentally, becoming childish, 'turning into a cabbage', if they did not struggle to keep their minds active:

> Some have coped very well; some have gone downhill mentally and physically. For example there was a man here who died last year: he became a cabbage; he and his cell were filthy. It is brought on by constant enclosure.

The remaining third seemed to think that some kinds of deteriorative effect was *inevitable*:

> (If you) keep people too long, they become institutionalised. I don't think they do cope. Life outside means problems and coping every day. In here, you live in a rut, you're a cabbage. You don't think; you go backwards and forwards like a mechanical doll.

However, many of this last group, while appearing to think the effects inevitable, also mentioned spontaneously, later in the interview, some action which they were themselves undertaking in order to combat them. Others who did not mention any deteriorative effects in answer to the direct question, did say that they themselves were deteriorating. Taking into account subjects' spontaneous self-descriptions, nearly half of the sample said that there was a risk of 'becoming a cabbage' but that the pressures in this direction could be resisted by the determined man, a quarter said that some kind of deterioration was inevitable and only a quarter did not mention deterioration at all.

This crucial element of awareness of pressure points the way to a reconciliation of the results with the psychological types of explanation given above. Awareness of pressure or of attempts to manipulate will very often distort predictions of behaviour because reactance is elicited. In the Wortman and Brehm paper it was suggested that a relatively mild constriction, provided the subject is aware of it, will produce reactance but that a more serious constriction produces learned helplessness. With the additional premise that the amount of reactance elicited (or the likelihood of it being elicited) will depend on the prior psychological state of the subject – which seems entirely plausible in view of the literature on 'locus of control' and on subjects' reactions to success and failure – the Wortman and Brehm synthesis would fit what happens in institutions. One would then say that a prison sentence, even of indeterminate length, is no insuperable blow to the prisoner's image of himself as basically in control of his life; it puts him under great pressure but he is able to find ways of dealing with the pressure, and reactance rather than helplessness is evoked. In more severely repressive conditions, such as concentration camps, the pressure is generally too great to be managed within the existing picture of the self, and the result is more often hopelessness and depression. Where the subject was already 'weak' and vulnerable to pressure (as with the three already inadequate lifers who failed to cope with their sentence) reactance would be less likely and helpessness more so – which would probably explain the larger number of 'institutionalized' patients in mental hospitals.

Stated simply, then, the outcome of this phase of the analysis is two amendments to the 'learned helplessness' approach to institutions developed above:

1. That 'deterioration' – i.e., the manifestations of learned helplessness – will occur only where the environment is extremely depriving or the inmate particularly vulnerable (or presumably with a combination of lesser values on both factors).
    AND
2. That lesser degrees of deprivation of control do not have their expected psychological effects on comparatively well-defended inmates, because 'reactance' is aroused and the inmate finds ways of reshaping or reperceiving the environment more in accord with his picture of himself and the world.

The hypothesis which was formally tested, however, stated simply that the life sentence would produce learned helplessness. The disproof of this contention does not establish the validity of the further *post hoc* conclusions; these were simply an attempt to make sense of apparently incompatible results. The conclusions are inherently suspect, as is all *post hoc* reformulation to save theory from the consequence of data. At their own level they have a certain plausibility. At another level, however, their neatness cast some doubt in my mind as to the relevance of the whole quantitative approach to the study of people's lives. It is this doubt which the rest of the book explores.

4

THE LIFER PROJECT II –
response and change

In Chapter 3 a model was derived, predominantly from the results of laboratory experimentation interpreted in the light of 'clinical' theories of anxiety and depression, which made predictions about how people will react to constraints on freedom and challenges to competence, depending on how radical the challenge or constraint turns out to be. The model argues that under circumstances which are tolerable, 'reactance' will be evoked as a 'healthy' or 'normal' defence: the subject will try harder to reassert freedom or competence or will try in some other way to preserve his centrally important picture of self as competent and in control. The lifer data reinforced this contention by failing to show deterioration or institutionalization but rather underlining the efforts prisoners put into reasserting personal control. (There were even several examples of men who had effectively *redefined* the environment in their minds and lives as one with greater possibilities for action than might at first appear.) Only when all else fails, because the environment is beyond toleration or because the subject is inherently vulnerable, would we expect to find 'helplessness', depression and ultimately the acceptance of self as powerless and incompetent.

There are conceptual problems with the account given in Chapter 3, however, even if it is evaluated on its own terms and within its own declared frame of reference, because it depends on a grossly extended interpretation of the concept of reactance. The original reactance experiments all measured subjects' declared or behaviourally expressed preferences for eliminated alternatives which they had expected to be free to choose. It has since been extended to cover any sudden change of attitude in resistance to social pressure (see Wicklund, 1974, for an extensive review) but it remains a 'motivational' theory of attitude change even in this wider formulation. The Wortman and Brehm paper discussed above stretches the concept to include hostile reactions to arbitrary attempts at control, de-emphasizing attitudes as criterion at the expense of behaviour. However, the concept still requires scope for action and measurable changes of motivation.

> . . . the motivational state of reactance . . . impells the person to reassert the freedom . . . There will always be forces moving the person in a direction opposite to the one implied by the threat. (Wicklund, 1974, p. 4)

> If someone . . . cannot of his own power bring some of these possibilities into play for himself, the concept of freedom is then irrelevant. (p. 1)

To explain the lifer work in terms of reactance requires a further stretching of the theory to allow that freedom may be 're-asserted' by a *cognitive* reconstruction of one's role and self-image and that a successful reconstruction abolishes the normal signs associated with reactance. It might validly be argued that this extension would attenuate the concept beyond its usefulness.

Beyond this, however, one may go on to question the frame of reference within which this *kind* of explanation is contained, and this is what I have increasingly found myself doing as I have worked over the data again and again. 'Helplessness' and 'reactance' are not actions or experiences of people; they are 'reactions of the organism'. When we stretch the scope of 'reactance' as a concept, it becomes not the reactance of the Brehm experiments but rather a shorthand term for explanations in terms of 'reasons', 'beliefs' and 'decisions'. Similarly, the 'picture of the world' in Chapter 3's model of human action is not a picture which anyone holds; it is a report of 'the state of the organism'. The longitudinal data described briefly in the chapter, however, suggests more a picture which a *person* can hold and share and work upon. A paradigm-shift to another kind of social psychology has occurred in the Lifer Project's afterlife of interpretation – from the psychology of what determines the organism's reactions to a psychology of how people cope and what they can do about their circumstances.

One of the first changes in my construction of the data was that I found myself coming to a far-reaching distrust of researchers' abstractions such as 'reactance', 'depression', 'learned helplessness' and the like, which are well founded in psychological theory but prescriptive rather than descriptive for the phenomenal field to which they are applied. Such concepts prescribe a model of man – man's behaviour is 'caused' by innate or more probably environmental factors. They prescribe an evaluative stance – behaviours and behavioural styles are to be treated as 'symptoms' of something or other, disorders to be cured. (This kind of over-psychologizing has been particularly prevalent in the criminological field, perhaps because of the seductive concept of 'penal *treatment*'.) They prescribe action: if behaviours are 'symptomatic' of 'disorders' then 'of course' they must be 'treated'; to suggest that interference with another's behaviour could involve ethical problems becomes like recommending that doctors refrain from treating broken legs. Finally, they prescribe exclusion-lines, and what is excluded is the possibility of considering what is found as the rational actions of thinking and feeling people.

Notions such as 'learned helplessness' and 'reactance' presume too much and place too great an emphasis on man as driven rather than driving – man as a thing to which environments happen, with predictable consequences – and this does not seem to me to be the only possible level of discourse for constructing psychological explanation. More important, they do not account for the *experience* of those with whom they are concerned: conscious analysis of situations, that most characteristically human of activities, is arbitrarily excluded from the scope of these models except as an irrelevant accompaniment to the 'true underlying processes'. Most important of all, the apparent simplicity conferred by this kind of reductionist analysis is wholly illusory. The simplicity and elegance of reductionist concepts can be maintained only by a constraint of the researcher's vision to those aspects of the situation where the pre-defined abstraction is most apt; to the extent that they are widened to cover more of the phenomena they lose their clarity of definition and begin to resemble metaphors more than they do explanatory concepts.

To an extent one may identify a 'new psychology' which has formed around the various dissatisfactions with the noble experiment of reductionist determinism, though it should be seen not so much as a movement, but rather as a range of overlapping concerns with humanity and human meaning. One of the important elements shared by all of this camp has been the stress on the person as active creator of meanings rather than as the passive channel between stimuli and responses. Throughout the history of social psychology both sides of the tension between man as the source of acts and man as passive until roused by stimulation from outside have been latent, but the latter strand has been far more fully developed. Social psychologists of recent years have been much concerned to reverse this trend and to reinstate agency as a central psychological concept:

> In early behaviourism, the antecedent events were presumed to be restricted to events in the outside world . . . Later, when such a crude model met with little explanatory success, . . . the place of organismic or 'intervening' variables came to be recognised. Now stimuli were . . . mediated in their effect by factors internal to the organism. But . . . whatever modifications were made to the basic model and however sophisticated the piece of machinery became that man was supposed to resemble the *paradigm* remained unchanged. Human beings continued to be regarded by psychologists as some kind of helpless clockwork puppet, jerked into life only when something happened to it. What is the alternative to this positivistic view of human behaviour? It is simply this . . . to credit human beings with the ability to be the causes of their own behaviour; to regard them, in other words, as *agents* . . . This is what we mean when we use the word 'person'; we refer to things that we know have the same ability as ourselves to intend their actions and to be aware what they are intending them. This is also how the word is meant when one proposes, as I am doing here, a *science of persons*.   (Heather, 1976, pp. 19–20)

Exactly this alternative constitutes the change of perspective from Chapter 3 to Chapter 4 in the present book. In Chapter 3 environmental pressures are conceptualized as *causing* prisoner behaviour; in Chapter 4 they are still seen as strong pressures, but the focus moves to how they are *construed* by the prisoners and what the prisoner *does* about them.

The importance of the 'picture of the world' has been given great weight in modern social psychology by the research and theorizing of George Kelly and his successors. Kelly's theory of how we build an understanding of our worlds is centred on the concept of man as an active agent rather than a passive 'receiver of stimuli'; he speaks not of *perception* but of *construction* or *construing*. In any given situation we are never without pre-conception; we come to every situation with a complete and moderately coherent picture of what the world is like and where we belong in it, based on past experience. The new situation is construed in the light of this picture – we form tentative or hypothetical judgements about what it means and make sense of it with reference to the general picture – and the judgements are tested when we 'behave' in the light of them and reconstrue the results of our actions. The similarities of this approach to the model proposed in Chapter 3 is obvious, but the underlying difference of approach is equally apparent: Chapter 3 talked of (predominantly automatic) *reactions* to stimulus situations, while the Kellian perspective talks of *action in response to understanding*.

An important corollary of this model is that the meaning of situations is not 'given in nature', but rather constructed by the person. This opens up the possibility that their meaning may be changed or 'reconstructed' by the person in order to render life more tolerable.

These 'pictures' cannot be taken altogether for granted, however, but need to be further located in the society in which the prisoner lives. It would be a mistake to isolate the meaning which an individual imposes on a situation and his or her personal history, forgetting that many of our 'personal meanings' are absorbed from others – we do not bring them with us at birth – and are implicit in the culture, structure and history of the wider society in which we live. This chapter, and indeed the research on which the whole book is based, tends more towards an individualistic style of explanation, but I have tried at the end of the chapter to indicate one way in which we may try to take the wider social world into account in our understanding of the individual's experience.

This chapter runs through several of the positions which recent humanistic and 'socio-cultural' psychologies have adopted. In the first section we take something akin to an action perspective, looking at what prisoners *do* to counteract the deprivation of personal property which imprisonment entails and how they reassert their control over time on an indeterminate sentence and give it some structure. The next section looks at the prisoner's efforts to assign an acceptable meaning to his situation. Section 3 explores the meaning of situations further, using Goffman's classification of responses to total institutions as a starting-point for a discussion of the overall 'stance' or 'style' which prisoners adopt to doing their sentence and how the nature of prison can be *changed* by the style which is adopted to cope with it. Finally, as an antidote to the simplistic voluntarism to which this kind of analysis is prone, we look at the origins of 'styles' in the material which the wider culture provides for us to use in constructing our identities.

4.1: *Doing something about deprivation*

The ways in which institution inmates cope with being deprived of personal property and of money are excellent illustrations of how people make reasonable lives for themselves piecemeal with the sparse materials to hand. When someone comes into an institution almost everything is taken away from him – his clothes, his toiletries, his books, his tools if he is a craftsman, his house and furniture and so on. Along with these *impedimenta* the prisoner loses the aspects of his public declared personality of which they are the marks or signs.

> It's as though it'd all been very carefully thought out as a deliberate way of humiliating you. First they write down all the details of you, then they take your personal possessions and seal them up in a packet, then they take your clothes off you and put them in a numbered box, and finally you end up standing there with just a towel round your waist. What they're doing is reducing your identity stage by stage, slowly wiping you out as a person until you're only one more piece of flesh with a name and number. It's frightening to have it done to you, to realise how easily it can be done, how completely powerless you are to prevent them taking away your individuality.   (a prisoner's account, in Parker (1973), p. 26)

Goffman notes of mental patients, and everyone notes of prisoners, that a great deal of effort is put into getting back a set of personal belongings, marking out a territory and coping in a world where by outside standards goods are in ludicrously short supply. Prison earnings are barely sufficient to keep a heavy smoker in tobacco, let alone to cover extra letters, newspapers, toiletries, books, handicraft equipment, birthday and Christmas cards, and food to supplement the doubtless nutritious but dull and lukewarm prison diet (which I tried for a couple of meals and would hesitate to recommend), and I saw the same kind of 'make do' expedients as Goffman describes – matches sliced into quarters with razor blades, cigarettes rolled needle-thin, prison garbage cannibalized as household utensils. (See also Foster, 1982, for a similar account of American prison experience.) Even those pieces of equipment which prison does provide are subject to official permission; one must ask the officer for a razor, or a sheet of notepaper, or to have the cell light on for an extra half hour at night, and that permission is often granted does nothing to diminish the feeling of powerlessness at having to ask.

In these circumstances, what meagre possessions can be established as one's own, and the marking out of a personal territory, take on a great importance. In all total institutions people come, as they acquire status, to have their own bunks, their own chairs, their own corner in the day room or area in the exercise yard, and these informal privileges or marks of status are jealously guarded. People take jobs in the prison laundry in order to be able to mark out a particular shirt as their own and give it special attention, or to have the informal privilege of changing their linen whenever they want to. People who are bedridden in long-stay hospitals hoard the most extraordinary things in their lockers – year-old newspapers, bits of string, half-eaten sandwiches. In Solzhenytsin's book *One Day in the Life of Ivan Denisovitch* we read how much possession of one's own knife or trowel was prized, and what a disaster it was when the guards found it and took it away; how much one prized possession of a pair of regulation boots which actually fitted, how much effort went into polishing them and keeping them supple, and what a blow it was when they had to be turned in and exchanged for summer shoes. (See also the role of illegally circulating literature in *The First Circle*.) This is not to be seen as blind acquisitiveness, nor purely as a matter of accumulating the goods that help physical survival; it is a reassertion of self in an environment which denies one control. In Bettelheim we read of concentration-camp inmates who would hoard a piece of wood or a stone, just for the pleasure and reassurance of owning something in a world where everything had been taken away. The hoarding behaviour of young children may perhaps be seen in a similar light, for they of all people have least privacy and least control over their world. (The similarities of situation between the prisoner and the young child are something of which the prisoners themselves are fully and explicitly conscious.)

Prisoners and people in mental hospitals do not have money and are not supposed to have free access to goods or services other than those provided and sanctioned by the institution; or if there is money, as in the prison where this research took place, there is not much of it. However, money is not just money, but a token exchangeable for goods and services and the exchange enlarges the liberty of both seller and buyer, because the seller chooses to sell and the buyer to buy; people can lead different and individual lives within a uniform institution if they can choose what goods and services they want. As a result, every institution has an illegal economic system with its own currency. Sometimes it is a simple barter system – people exchange sausages, of which they are not fond, for chips or bacon which they like. Normally it is more formal, with an agreed medium of exchange – occasionally a true currency, as with the concentration-camp paper money described by Radford (1945, pp. 196 ff) whose value was determined by *fiat*, but more often one of the available commodities of the institution. Tobacco is the normal medium of exchange in this country or America, in prisons, but other things can fulfil the same role. In certain prisons stamp-collecting and budgerigar-breeding have caused problems on occasions: both stamps and young budgerigars are portable and highly valued by long-term prisoners, giving them a value as currency, but both are in short supply, so that debts are very difficult to meet – a situation paralleling periods in European history when coinage was in very short supply among the peasantry.

One should of course note that this kind of economic adaptation is not unique to prisons and other institutions but is also to be found in the outside world, though not to the same extent or with the same importance attached to it. People in factories or offices, doing boring routine jobs, acquire property and territory. They have their own workbench, their own tools, their own desk, their own table in the library (or their usual table), their own pen or pencil, their own chair in the canteen, their own cup at the tea trolley, a time when they have priority in the queue for the loo, a time when they knock off work and have a cup of coffee. Some of these are actually 'property', issued by the management. Some are privileges or customs which have just grown up. Nonetheless they are jealously guarded and can be seen as a way of acquiring control and a personal stake in a world which essentially belongs to someone else.

Time is another of the great deprivations of prison, and particularly of indeterminate sentences. It is taken for granted within our culture (but very much a culture-specific way of conceptualizing it) that time is a measurable and expendable or tradable commodity – as Smith (1961) puts it, 'a commodity to be spent, lost, invented, saved, wasted, thrown away or employed to best advantage':

. . . time ticks away relatively unobserved and unanalysed. We
talk of it chiefly as a resource – we do not have enough of it, we
cannot spare any of it for visits to our relations, we must make
some so that we can squeeze in this or that activity. We can turn
down any engagement on the grounds that we 'simply have no
time' and we can become irritated by those who waste time or
have time 'on their hands' without using it. (Cohen and
Taylor, 1972, p. 97)

In another sense of the word, we measure ourselves against time
in the way that a racer does: the successful man has completed a
lap in so many months or years, while the unsuccessful may
never reach a certain point of the course, however long they take
and however much effort they expend. (This is an oversimplifi-
cation, of course, but the metaphor is a valid one.) From both of
these senses of how our culture conceptualizes time life-
sentence prisoners are potentially excluded to their grave
psychological disadvantage.

They have 'all the time in the world' because prison time is
endless and empty. We have all developed ways of thought and
action which protect us from the existential uncertainty of
simple inactive being – 'flow activities', to use the term coined
by Csikzentmihalyi (1976) – and prison takes these away along
with the prisoner's clothes and possessions. The prison day is
essentially empty, and one day closely resembles another:

> Due to a general lack of interest
> Tomorrow has been cancelled
> And in its place will be
> A continuous repetition of today
> Which may be very monotonous
> But definitely seems to be
> In response to public demand

to quote a poem by a man serving eight years, reproduced by
Parker (1973). Time is something to be served, survived, 'lived
through' but in no real sense 'lived'. Prison time is an interrup-
tion of life, not a part of it, like a form of cryogenic suspension
through which the patient remains fully conscious, and there
are nearly four thousand potentially near-identical days in even
the 'average' life sentence, each filled with one thousand, four
hundred and forty-four minutes.

At another level the prisoner has no time at all because his
own time has been taken away from him by the courts – he has
potentially no personal future that can be planned or anti-

cipated in the mind, having been sentenced to a prison future
for what could conceivably turn out to be the rest of 'his' life:

> It's difficult in visits, we don't talk much about the future: I
> don't suppose we have one. What can I say to her? 'When I get
> out of here, in ten years – or perhaps twelve – or perhaps fifteen –
> or perhaps . . .' I don't suppose she'll stick with me, and I
> couldn't blame her if she didn't. It's not fair on her. It's no life
> for her, is it?

The prisoner has to live with potentially no sense of direction,
movement or purpose, which is a constraint beyond the scope of
our culture's repertoire of normal-life adaptations.

For a few, this potential becomes an actuality, as they sink
into a world with no substance and no future. One cannot but
be amazed, however, at the power of human beings to cope, and
where there is no clear future most humans will still somehow
construct one. How people deal with the anxiety consequent on
indeterminate commitment is most movingly described by
Julius Roth (1963) in his book on the ways in which he and
other patients dealt with their time in tuberculosis hospitals:

> . . . people will not accept uncertainty. They will make an effort
> to structure it no matter how poor the materials they have to
> work with and no matter how much the experts try to discour-
> age them. One way to structure uncertainty is to structure the
> time period through which uncertain events occur.

He refers to this process as 'drawing up timetables' and com-
pares the structure thus imposed on indeterminacy to the
common-language conception of 'a career'. Much of his book is
about how TB patients bargain with their doctors to establish
the length and pattern of this 'career', which is not of a great
relevance to the study of lifers (whose opportunities for bargain-
ing are somewhat limited, to say the least), but his notions of the
reference point or 'benchmark' and the reference group fit very
closely to what lifers do with 'life'.

The 'benchmarks' of which he speaks are reference points
which the TB patient uses as signs of how far he or she has
progressed along the hospital career towards release back into
ordinary society – e.g., hospital classifications, 'privileges' such
as being allowed up, aspects of diagnosis and treatment such as
X-ray appointments. Over and above the 'grand timetable' of norms which all patients of a given hospital had worked
out for themselves, Roth also found expectations of norms for

sub-groups within the hospital, and it was extremely important for patients to find a group within which their own case could be located as 'typical'; the more specific timetable of the sub-group gave them something with which they could compare their own progress. Moreover:

> The choice of which patients to compare himself with does not necessarily remain static throughout a patient's stay in the hospital . . . When the doctors start 'talking surgery' to a patient, he will consider the experience of others who had surgery and that of apparently similar (to him) cases in which the patient refused surgery in order to decide . . . which is the lesser evil from his viewpoint. If he does decide to accept surgery, he will then focus his attention primarily on the experience of other surgery patients in an effort to predict what will happen to him.   (p. 18)

The location of oneself differentially within one or another group of patients must also be a two-way process: one uses the norm for the group to measure one's own progress, but by the same token the fact that one appears to be moving faster or slower than the group may be an indication that another group's timetable may be more appropriate.

The same kind of process was evident among life-sentence prisoners. Most of the ones I interviewed knew what the average life sentence was, plus or minus a year, and they knew which categories tended to stay longer or less than the average. The assessments of their own probable term made by men who were not at the very beginning of sentence were generally consistent with the factors known to relate to term served. (This was not always the case – the man might seize on some features of his case which is in fact unlikely to affect the releasing authorities and predict a long sentence for himself because of it – but it is very often so.) They also knew how to interpret changes of prison or changes of job within the prison; these are in fact signals of progress which have been worked out, tacitly, between Prison Department and the prisoners, intended to convey information about progress without committing the Department to a verbal promise or release on a certain date (as such a promise is not within the Department's power to make.) Seeking for information about progress is a way, in a sense, of asserting control and negating helplessness; to know what is going on at least makes one *feel* less helpless, and it may show what one should be doing to speed things up. The authorities in the individual prisons are also likely to provide at least some semblance of landmarks.

> Neither we nor they can cope with the sentence if we think of it as a straight line. So we build in artificial stages – some formal (deriving from Home Office procedures), some typical of the particular institution, some traditional in a particular Wing even.   (A prison governor)

Some, of course, would claim to have no knowledge whatsoever of how long the sentence might be expected to last or of what kinds of factor might influence the decision, comparing it rather to a lottery or some kind of 'Act of God'. Typical of such responses is the one which Tony Parker has reproduced in his 1973 anthology:

> No, I've no idea how they decide when to let you out. One prisoner told me the thing to do was behave very badly for about five years and then start to behave better, so they'd think you were making progress. Another one said it was best to be a model prisoner right from the start. Then you meet someone who's done just that and you find he's been in fifteen years so far and still's got no idea when he's going out, and another chap who's been a bloody nuisance and that everybody hates and suddenly you find he's given a release date . . . So don't ask me: for all I know the system might be drawing numbers out of a hat.

Very many men said something like this to me at some point in the interview – generally near the start or in response to a direct question about release procedures – but from the records of their conversation during the rest of the interview it was clear that nearly all of them were able to mobilize some idea about what the procedures were.

For instance, most lifers are in fact aware that release is partly a medical or quasi-medical decision (you are not released until you are 'fit for release' – i.e. when the authorities are satisfied you will not re-offend), partly a political one (taking into account press reactions, the notoriety of the case and the vociferousness of relatives of the victim), and almost totally beyond the control of the prisoner. About a third of the sample regarded it as arbitrarily awarded by the Home Office or the Parole Board (they generally confuse the two), citing particular cases to prove the absence of rationale. Another fifth thought it depended on the nature of the crime and the psychiatric reports, neither of which elements is much open to manipulation. Two men said they thought release might be brought forward if influential people outside made life hell for the Home Secretary, but not otherwise. Time already served was apparently not related to what was believed.

How, then, does one structure indeterminacy in the absence of a goal that one believes attainable or a terminal date in which one has confidence? To some extent the problem is made easier by the presence of landmarks deliberately built into the system by Prison Department under a new system of 'lifer management' introduced not long before the lifer sample was selected. Prison moves and allocation of prison work have long been landmarks for the lifer: moves from 'harder' to 'softer' prisons were interpreted as signs of progress (not always with good justification, particularly in the case of men likely to serve very long terms), and transfer to Leyhill (an 'open' prison) or to a job outside the prison walls was a sign that release was at least being contemplated. As an assistant governor said to me:

> At four years there is almost a kind of contentment – no, not contentment, more relaxation. By the time he's done four years he can more or less work it out: say he is to serve ten years; he'll be six months at hostel, two or three years at Leyhill, with probably a period working outside before that: that leaves only two years to struggle with. He's broken the sentence down into manageable periods.

With the introduction of formal security categorization in 1966, downgrading of category became another visible sign of progress. Now, under the 'revised management strategy', the life sentence is conceived much more as a planned career. After an 'assessment' period of three years at one of two large prisons, lifers are to progress through a series of planned moves, probably at intervals of two or three years, and probably in most cases from higher- to lower-security prisons: more low-security places for lifers have been provided to make this possible. At the same time more attention is being given to planning work and education for the whole career, with the prisoner participating in the planning. (To some extent the 'signs of progress' are illusory, in that Prison Department is not the releasing authority and cannot guarantee release in a particular year, but it is generally possible to estimate at least the minimum likely duration of the sentence.)

When asked a series of specific questions about where they thought they might be moved next and how they would react to a move to various types of prison, about 50 per cent of the lifer sample appeared thoroughly conversant with the new system and two thirds conversant with at least the broad outlines. Among those aware of the system, the 'breaking up' of the sentence mentioned by the assistant governor is a very evident process:

> I expect I shall be moved to another prison sometime between December and March (the Open University finishes in October to November). I should get a review in the next twelve months. I suppose I will go to an open prison in three or four years' time. I don't want to work outside the prison; I'm not interested in gardening.

> I expect I'll carry on bricklaying until I get outside work at, say, six years. I don't think they'll move me to another prison. I'm coming up for review fairly soon anyway. Perhaps I might go to an Open Prison in the last year or eighteen months, and then perhaps to a hostel for the last six months, although an Open Prison is more or less like a hostel.

> I hope to learn a trade: engineering probably. Education. To build up my cell hobbies and read books. I'm here for four years. Then I should get a review in another three. I suppose I'll go to an open prison or a hostel nearer release.

Even among those who did not appear aware of the role of open prisons, hostels and working outside, many had the concept of progress towards release through a hierarchy of prisons – for example: 'The next move must be on a par with this one, not a step back like going, say, to Parkhurst.'

For some, the main line of the lifer career is something to which they cannot realistically aspire or from which they have already departed by their failure to achieve serious consideration for release and, as Roth points out,

> There must be some provision in every career for those who cannot keep up to the mark, especially those who are being left hopelessly behind to the point where they become a class apart.

In each of Roth's TB hospitals there was a 'chronic ward' peopled by those whose condition was showing no sign of improvement and who were therefore 'stuck' or 'blocked' in their promotion, where privileges would be awarded them in the light of their 'long-stay status' which carried no implication of progress towards health:

They are still patients, but receiving largely maintenance care rather than active treatment. They are still part of the domain occupied by their career group, but no longer part of the forward moving promotion system.

Similarly there are lifers in respect of whom the staff no longer see their task as preparation for release but as the provision of maintenance activities to prevent deterioration.

A final note: Roth describes physicians and surgeons as having just the same kind of conception of the TB patient's stay in hospital as a career as the patient does, but with more information because they are themselves responsible for the decisions. In prison, similarly, both staff and prisoners conceptualize the sentence as a career; indeed, the former may even suggest this conceptualization to the latter on occasion, as a way of getting through the sentence intact. The staff whom the prisoner actually meets, however, are closer to the patient's position than the physician's in terms of the information they possess. They may be recommending release but they do not determine it, and positive recommendations are frequently turned down, at least in the first instance. Staff, like prisoners, are therefore in the position of having to guess the likely outcome of remote Parole Board or Home Office proceedings.

4.2: *Coming to terms and responding to circumstance*

One very noticeable common feature in all accounts of total institutions is the grave emotional disturbance which is to be seen in the early months after reception, consequent on disrupted lifestyle. (Many institutions have formal 'induction phases' which might appear purposely designed to mark the disruption and aggravate the disturbance, and prison's 'reception routines' may readily be seen as fulfilling this function.) The sample of lifers in the current study were far from exempt from these problems. We saw in the last chapter that most lifers go through a phase of anxiety, depression, withdrawal and/or belligerence as they try to come to terms with their new situation. Previous experience is obviously an important variable here. Lawton (1978) found that it was the men without much previous experience of imprisonment who appeared most concerned with the trivial details of day-to-day living in prison and most distressed by them, while more experienced men tended to complain more about broader issues such as autonomy or communication. Similarly, men with a history of past prison sentence were less likely to show certain kinds of initial disturbance than 'naive' subjects.

Coming to terms with the offence which has been committed may be as difficult a problem for the offender as coming to terms with prison. The experience of hearing the life sentence passed and of coming into prison may be extremely disturbing: 'I was new to it. I thought I would be in prison for ever', a man who had been inside for five or six years said to me about his reception, and this would appear to be a fairly typical reaction. More disturbing still, however, is the nature of the offence itself. The public stereotype of the killer is not a sympathetic role and the fact of the action may well be very difficult to integrate into one's self-concept.

To obtain information on so personal and so well guarded a topic as a lifer's offence is very difficult indeed. Direct questioning is liable to produce results deliberately distorted by the subject (if indeed he is aware of and able to formulate his own feelings, which one may doubt), and to rely on staff reports is merely to confound this same problem, with that of unknown interviewer bias. In the interviews I carried out with the lifers, however, no questions were asked about the offence, so that what subjects said about it of their own accord may provide some clues to the process of coming to terms with it. In the newly-received group I found that about half expressed feelings categorizable as remorse or regret, and a quarter did not mention the offence at all during the interview; by the time mid-sentence is reached, the proportion who do not mention the offence has doubled, while only a third mentioned it with remorse or regret. (The 'hard-core' group will not bear much interpretation, as I interviewed only six people, but we might note that two of these six felt they needed psychiatric help to understand their offences, compared with three out of the remaining fifty; it should be remembered that sex offenders are heavily over-represented in the hard core.)

Each offence-type presents its own distinct pattern. The majority of the men whose crime involved theft did not mention it in interview, and only one man expressed any marked degree of remorse. In the 'domestic' category (killers of wives, mistresses, girlfriends, own children, other family, wife's lover, etc.) 70 per cent express remorse or regret and most of these are properly classed as remorse; typically the wife-killers said they could never forgive themselves for what they had done and that they had 'killed their world'. Among men whose crime showed sexual features about 40 per cent expressed remorse or regret, and another 40 per cent did not mention the offence. Most of the remaining sex cases said they needed psychiatric help, a smaller proportion than one might have predicted (as this is a classic way of denying responsibility) but the largest group to do so. Remarkably few men claimed to be innocent – mostly men at the beginning of sentence whose offences do not fall in the 'sex' or 'domestic' categories. (The distribution of attitudes by age, which was also examined, yielded nothing of any significance.)

One of the men whose crime was recorded as one of attempted rape followed by murder was much concerned, when I interviewed him, to deny the sexual element:

> On remand, I lied, and tried to get away with it. The sentence hasn't bothered me, frankly, so much as what I've done. The police put together the official story and it isn't really what happened. I was convicted of strangling a woman in the course of indecent assault. What really happened: I got off the bus with a woman, having drunk a bit, and I fancied her. We talked. We walked down a lane, and I made a pass, perhaps got some encouragement. She returned my kiss. Then suddenly she said she was 'on the rag' (menstruating); I insulted her about leading me on: she slapped and scratched me, belting me with her handbag; I hit her on the nose, she went hysterical. I put my arms around her neck and told her to shut up. She fell down marking a gargling noise. I thought at first she was having me on. Then she was stiff. I thought she was unconscious. There was no pulse. I opened her blouse to listen to her heart; she was dead. It wasn't a psychological thing, just violent loss of temper. I regret it bitterly; I would like to repay.

From the man's manner and the way he launched into this subject before any questions had been asked it was evident that he believed this account and felt very strongly about it. It may be a true account, though the very detailed police evidence contradicts several details of the story. If false it would be an excellent example of how one may come to terms with part of a past action by changing its character in memory.

In four cases there was no report of initial disturbance due to either the offence or entry into the prison, whether in interview or on the documents prepared during the first year of sentence. For two of them it appears that prison was rendered tolerable by a combination of previous experience and outside ties. The one, who has served a substantial prison sentence in the past and was a sailor for much of his early life, was the only truly professional criminal in the sample. He and his wife accept prison sentences as a normal risk for him and his declared intention is simply to get through the sentence as quickly and as sensibly as he can and return to his family; he regards the sentence simply as an irrelevant interval to be lived through and then forgotten. The second has no record of imprisonment, but he was six years in the army and spent another four as a civilian clerk in one of the services. His wife and children, from whom he was estranged, saw the reports of his arrest on television and re-established a contact which is proving enormously helpful to him in dealing with his sentence: 'I think I'd crack up if I didn't have my family.' A third man was also sustained by regular family contact, and he was still in process of appealing against both conviction and sentence; not yet accepting the sentence as an irreversible fact, he had not yet been required to come to terms with it.

The fourth man, 'Brian Caine' (the name is of course fictitious) shows a different pattern. In interview he admits that the sentence was 'hard' at first but says that it gets no easier as time goes on, and his life outside is not remembered as having been a happy one. He had little previous experience of prison – only two very short sentences – but he has always been a rootless and solitary individual, something of a displaced person. He left his family in Ireland during his teens and came to England to find work; contact with his natal family was lost at that point and has never been re-established. In the years prior to his offence he is described as a rootless and friendless man, with no known female acquaintances, a heavy drinker with an unstable work history. Medical staff do not record anxiety as characteristic of his early period specifically, but as chronic in him. He has always been an anxious and emotionally unstable man, since long before he came into prison, and he remains so now after serving more than ten years.

With these four exceptions every lifer in the sample showed a period of emotional 'floundering' as he tried to come to terms with the sentence and with his future and to integrate the fact of having murdered into a viable picture of the self. (For some, particularly those who had killed a wife or other 'object of love', the fact of having murdered appeared a harder challenge than the conditions of the prison.) In varying degrees and with varying rapidity this period dies away, however, and most men come to know the prison environment and to build a temporary life within it.

Among the ten men in the 'hard core' group there were three who failed to cope altogether – to find and maintain a viable 'style':

1. 'Michael Smith' (again the name is fictitious) was convicted at the age of forty of the murder of a bystander who intervened during a quarrel with his ex-wife. At reception medical staff reported considerable depression and neuroticism coupled with a violent temper. Other staff found that he settled in quickly, spending a fair amount of time in his cell doing hobby activities but also mixing freely and attracting good reports at his work. Up to about year seven he continued so, but in the eighth year a change set in, going through withdrawal to acute depression and a suicide attempt for which he was hospitalized. Later, after injuring another prisoner severely in a trivial argument, he was recommended for transfer to a 'special hospital' under a diagnosis of psychotic depression. However, no bed was found for him there and after several years the transfer instruction was cancelled. He remains in the prison hospital, and latest reports describe him as temperamental, prone to depressions and liable to come into confrontation with staff.

2. 'Richard Bacon' was convicted at the age of thirty-five of the sexual murder of a child. At reception he was judged to be of low intelligence though not actually subnormal, and psychologists speak of him as having an unrealistic and pathetic assessment of his own abilities, a complete inability to mix with people of his own age and a tendency to project all his difficulties onto other people. Immediately after reception he experienced a great deal of trouble from other inmates. This died down fairly quickly, but his *fear* of other inmates grew from year to year, to the point where it was said that one glance from another inmate was enough to send him scurrying to an officer for protection. In his sixth year he was hospitalized after a suicide attempt, and he has been there ever since; he declares openly that he will never go back into the main prison. At one time he kept his mind busy with hobbies, but in the last four or five years television has been his only occupation.

3. 'Richard Scott' was convicted in his late teens of murdering a woman in the course of sexual assault. His behaviour – labile, uncontrolled and prone to passive homosexuality even at reception – deteriorated steadily during the first ten years of sentence. Depression built up, and he went from a child-like dependence on staff to active and destructive homosexuality, theft, dirtying of his cell and threats of suicide. He was sent to Grendon Underwood (the psychiatric prison) for therapy, but with no marked effects. At the end of this period he was described as 'unwashed, unkempt and thoroughly disliked by both staff and inmates'. In his eleventh year he underwent brain surgery and there was a marked change in his behaviour – he became cooperative and eager to please and began to make great efforts to demonstrate his fitness for release. Subsequent reports suggest alternation between hope for the future and depressive despair, in cycles of several months.

These three could not settle to a viable lifestyle in prison; two of them never found one at all. All three broke down into a condition described by doctors as pathological. It seems fairest, however, to describe prison as the place where they broke down rather than as the cause of the break. None of them had 'made a success' of their lives outside. Smith had a long record of past convictions, eight or nine periods in prison etc., a correspondingly poor work record and a broken marriage. Bacon was an itinerant labourer with a broken marriage and no ability to form even casual friendships. Scott, in his late teens, was described as obsessed with sex but knowing little about it and quite incapable of normal social contacts; he had several convictions for indecent assault. One should also note that none of the three had much to go out to after release. Scott had only a mother, who ceased to answer his letters after he had been in for six years. Smith had a sister, but his mother died in the fifth year of his sentence. Bacon had nobody.

Apart from these three, all of the sample found a way of dealing acceptably with the sentence. Looking at staff reports a clear distinction is apparent between men whose activities are directed chiefly at planning for the time after their release, those whose activity is seen as purely 'internal to the prison' – men who are climbing the ladder of prison jobs and privileges, or becoming expert at prison 'fiddles', or undertaking an educational programme or a hobby task purely for its own sake – and a third group who appear to be just waiting out their sentence and making no plans. A small fourth group may also be distinguished – among the newly-received men – who are still preoccupied with appeals and have not yet come to terms with prison as an inescapable reality. One such was mentioned earlier in the chapter and Toch (1975) speaks of others who have made it their prison career:

> Anyone who has been around prisons has seen inmates who spend years working on transparently fruitless legal appeals, which had the combined virtue of keeping busy and nurturing hope. I remember one inmate . . . who finally committed suicide and whose psychological decline began when he stopped doing 'legal work'.

(I would not presume to consider any of the appeals initiated by men in my sample 'transparently fruitless' but the stratagem is presumably even more effective as a way of structuring time if it has at least some realistic chance of succeeding.)

The first of these classes, who are 'working for release', might be typified by one man of whom it is written that:

> His aim is to go on full-time education as soon as possible, taking an 'A' level course and hopefully going on to a degree. Feels his occupation in the future will depend on what sort of certificates he manages to gain while in prison.

Another:

> Has completed a Painters' VTC and is now on full-time book education . . . is determined to work towards release. Is working for open prison: sees this as something of a delaying tactic but a step in the right direction.

Typical of the 'prison oriented' class would be a man of whom a prison officer writes that he: 'Spends his free time drawing, painting and reading – also he has some ambition to write songs and even a book'; or the convoluted attempts at impression management of another man who wanted a comfortable 'red band' job. Of other men, however, staff say that: 'He gives the impression of being quite happy just drifting along.' or: 'It would seem that during his first four years he decided that time simply had to be passed and that there was little requirement on him to do anything positive.'

The comments of prisoners during interview do not fall

naturally into the same categories as the comments of staff; a much more salient dimension for them was their attitude to the work, education and training facilities provided by the authorities. About 30 per cent were either using one of these facilities as a way of structuring the sentence and feeling they were doing something useful or were awaiting the opportunity to do so. Several men were pursuing courses provided by the prison establishment, but courses are by no means the only available facility: 'The main thing is to keep your mind occupied. That's why I'm in the kitchens, for something to do. It's creative.'

About a quarter preferred to fall back on their own resources, undertaking private education programmes or hobby work:

> Now, since I've been involved in education and cell hobbies, I've never looked back. I have been studying the Bible. I have won thirty two certificates on Bible courses in the last eighteen months . . . I am also doing art full time; I never stop. It's the best way for me to pass the time. I am looking into the history of print making. I won an award last year . . . I do my sentence in 'two year plans'. I did two years of weaving; then lino-cuts; now I'm turning over to woodcuts. I haven't watched television since 1969.

This is admittedly an extreme example of deliberate planning and the segmenting of time, but many not much less extreme could be quoted. A smaller but still substantial group did not fall in either of these categories but were vociferous about the need for better work or educational classes or some other way of marking progress:

> You should have a chance to make something of yourself earlier on; trade training should be dealt with much earlier in sentence.

> There ought to be a better system of work. The longer you do, the better you ought to get . . . For example, you should get kitchens as a privilege . . . There used to be a 'stage earnings' system. You worked towards something. At three years you got a radio, at three and a half curtains, passed out or red band at seven or eight years. That was a thoroughly good system. Now you get it all on the first day and from there it's downhill all the way.

Finally, about a quarter made no comment relevant to the topic in the whole course of a long interview and may therefore be presumed to be uninterested in it.

Men with previous institutional experience and men early in sentence were most likely to be aligned to prison facilities and men with no institutional experience least likely, but the differences are not large. Larger differences are to be seen when classifying by 'offence-type': 50 per cent of the 'theft' and 'domestic' cases were oriented towards a prison-provided facility, compared with only one in ten of the men whose crimes showed sexual features; these last were somewhat more likely than others to be pursuing self-directed activities, possibly because these kept them out of the threatening company of other prisoners. Age had little effect, except that men over forty were less likely to mention such activities at all, and the stability or otherwise of the man's past work history in the outside world was also unrelated to his present attitude.

This section of the chapter has looked briefly at what prisoners do to render the prison environment tolerable – their responses to the prison environment. A study of how people cope in my own institution, the Open University, would probably show much the same: some people concerned with activities which will establish them in their professions and extend the range of outside jobs for which they may apply, others fervently engaged in University politics and University management, furthering their career *within* the institution, others who are just 'doing the job', and probably a small fourth class who have not yet managed to make sense of the place. What prisoners do in prison is what anyone does anywhere.

What is specific to prison is not the activities undertaken but the importance which they assume as carriers and preservers of sanity and self-concept. Prison offers the prisoner very little material out of which to construct an 'everyday' life and so prison life lacks the 'redundancy' of layers of self-protection to which we are normally accustomed. In ordinary life we can try, fail and be free to try again without having to acknowledge ultimate failure. If things are going wrong in one sphere of life, another may offer compensation – failures at work, for example, may be compensated by satisfactory experience of home and family. Prison life is 'thin', however – the total institution does not offer distinct 'spheres of life' – and the prisoner must 'get it right' or suffer more severe consequences to self-image than is generally the case in the outside world.

4.3:   *Styles of adaptation*

The dominant and most obvious single strategem of prison life
is that of simply *coping* with the environment, getting through
without trouble, just killing time until release. A multiplicity of
prison studies might be cited in support of this statement. Sykes
(1958), for instance, notes as primary objective of all prison
inmates (both prisoners and staff) the maintenance of a quiet
prison. Glaser (1964), similarly, proposes that 'a predominant
interest to prison inmates is to adjust to the expectations of their
keepers in order to stay out of trouble while confined'. Irwin
(1970) covers the same notion with his 'doing time' stereotype:

> . . . they come into prison and 'do their time'. They attempt to
> pass through this experience with the least amount of suffering
> and the greatest amount of comfort. They (1) avoid trouble, (2)
> find activities which occupy their time, (3) secure a few luxuries,
> (4) with the exception of complete isolates, form friendships
> among small groups of other convicts, and (5) do whatever they
> think is necessary to get out as soon as possible.

Morris and Morris (1961, pp. 350–54) also discuss this way of
dealing with prison life in Pentonville under the headings of
'ritualism', 'manipulation' and 'prisonized withdrawal', and
King and Elliott (1977) have aspects of it as a common theme in
the various styles of adaptation which they describe in Albany.
(See also Flanagan (1981) for an account of coping as a 'long-
term prisoner perspective'.) However much one may detect
grand 'strategies of adaptation', it remains true that most of the
prisoner's daily effort is expended on the day-to-day tactics of *ad
hoc* coping.

A case in point among the 'hard-core' group and one who has
not exactly 'adjusted to the expectations of his keepers' is
'Robert Kershaw'. On reception Kershaw was described by
prison officers as clean, tidy and a good influence because
of his quiet and mature manner, well behaved but not always
obedient to orders. He was a keen chess player and appeared to
enjoy association with selected other prisoners. His work
supervisor described him as keen and as having the makings of a
first-class machinist. At the beginning of his sentence he was in
correspondence with his wife and mother, and both visited
regularly. His wife divorced him in the third year of sentence,
however, and despite strenuous efforts he was not able to maintain contact with his children. Thereafter his behaviour and

attitudes began to change: he became supercilious and obstructive with staff and indifferent to other inmates. He is reported as saying that he knew he could not 'beat the system', but that it satisfied him to try and might help him to get through the sentence. A year or so later he began to show depressive symptoms, for which valium was prescribed. For the next five years he had recurrent periods of anxiety and depression during which he tended to be uncooperative with staff, though not a discipline problem. His main activities were solitary or conducted in small groups – chess, television, listening to classical music. At the time of the interview attempts had been made to prepare him for future release by cutting off his tranquilizers and giving him work outside the prison. However his behaviour became erratic – not unremarkably after more than five years on drugs – and he declined outside work until he had a firm date for release. In interview he told me he knew he was 'cutting off his nose to spite his face', but his pride would not allow him to accept more half-promises and he saw no good reason for cutting his standard of living. He described the last ten years as 'just coasting on, trying to stay fit and avoid depression'.

With the proviso that most prisoners spend most of their time 'just coping' (or occasionally failing to cope), there is nonetheless some understanding to be gained by trying to classify the general 'stance' or 'style', which prisoners have adopted to cope with their terms. Goffman (1957, 1961), in his classic observational study of life in mental hospitals, distinguishes four styles of adaptation practised by patients: 'colonization', 'conversion', 'intransigence' and 'situational withdrawal'. This may serve as a starting-point for the discussion.

In colonization, which has loosely been compared with 'institutionalization' by some, the subject gives up all expectation of ever getting out, turns his back on the outside world and makes a life for himself in the prison or hospital. He tends to think only about his life inside and how to make it comfortable and meaningful; he makes plans and thinks ahead, but with a view only to rising within the institution and increasing his control of his environment, not with release and a life outside in mind. He may well use his knowledge of life inside to point contrasts with the outside world in the institution's favour. This is said to be a common adaptation to the long-stay wards of mental hospitals and in old people's homes, where it is quite a rational strategy – the inmates are not going anywhere, so they might as well make the best of what they have. (See also Shiloh,

1971, for exemplary cases.) Even in extreme conditions, such as the Nazi concentration camps, inmates who survived came somehow to 'make a life' in the camps and the stratagem of colonization was to be observed among some of the men who had been there longest. So much did motivation change that 'colonized' prisoners were not above killing men in their own group who fell ill, in order to prevent punishment of the whole group. (See also Newman, 1944, for a brief account of 'colonizing' in prisoner of war camps.)

A few of the lifers showed some signs of colonization, but there was only one relatively pure case of it – 'Reginald Hayward' in the 'hard-core' group. Reg Hayward killed a young boy at the age of thirty-five, in the course of a sexual assault; he had ten previous convictions (several of them similar to the present one but not involving violence), had been twice in prison and once in a mental hospital. He had held down a series of labouring jobs in the outside world, none lasting as long as six months, and was married but the relationship was a poor and unstable one. On reception he showed some enthusiasm for classes and trade training, but he proved unable to cope with them, and since then he has spent his whole sentence 'in the background', perfectly adapted, as successive staff reports show:

> (Year 3) Work effort satisfactory . . . a quiet lonely man who unless one looks for him is liable to remain unnoticed . . . seems to get on well enough.
> (Year 6) Vegetates . . . Still in his shell and does not come to notice.
> (Year 8) Is reluctant to take on anything more demanding. Never participates . . . Appears happy and undisturbed with his pattern of life.
> (Year 10) Still in the same routine job. Does not engage in communal activity and has no academic pursuits.
> (Year 12) Remains very much of a nonentity. Pathetically institutionalised.

The high point of his prison career came a year or so before I saw him, when he was appointed cleaner to one of the prison social workers; this gave him his own specific territory and made him very happy. In interview he admitted to having almost forgotten what the outside world was like and to having become afraid of it.

Overall, however, one would have to say that colonization

was a rare style among lifers. Most lifers remain too concerned with release and too hopefull that prison is a passing stage even if its passing is long delayed and subject to arbitrary refusal, to be compelled to think of prison as a home. Generally the men who colonized had few outside ties and little or nothing to look forward to in the outside world. Hayward's total outside contacts, for example, amounted to the occasional exchange of cards with his elderly father.

The kind of condition which this research originally set out to examine – e.g., Barton's 'institutional neurosis' – is more closely paralleled by Goffman's 'institutional withdrawal', where:

> The inmate withdraws apparent attention from everything except events immediately around his body and sees these in a perspective not employed by others present . . . drastic curtailment or involvement in interactional events . . . (Goffman, 1961)

Methods of achieving the same effect have been observed and described by a number of authors. For example, one case of it was noted by Caudill *et al* (1952) even in an open and socially integrated ward for relatively mild neurotic cases; they speak of:

> . . . the complete isolation imposed on himself by Mr. Reed (who), though physically present on the ward, never entered the social field of the patients. (p. 326)

Withdrawal into the immediate situation was not uncommon among the lifers in this sample during some part of the first year or so of sentence, but thereafter it was again an uncommon form of adaptation. A very few prisoners exhibited it to a pathological degree – those who 'broke' during sentence and retreated into schizophrenia. One man, for example, is described as interacting with neither prisoners nor staff: he spends his time wandering round the prison wing muttering to himself and scavenging cigarette ends. A few more may be said to exhibit some feature of the style – some men in the 'hard-core' group, for example – but here I am not inclined to consider the stance pathological because it is deliberately and rationally adopted. Even in this milder form institutional withdrawal was very uncommon among prisoners earlier in sentence than the 'hard-core' cases except as a transitory way of coping with particular disappointments.

The third of Goffman's strategies, intransigence, is rare in prison because counter-productive. It cannot lead to release or enlargement of liberty in this setting and is thus self-defeating. Some men are intransigent in their early years. One or two of the 'hard-core' group, for instance, spent a long time trying to bludgeon their way through the prison system and did not begin to show visible signs of cooperation with the authorities until around the 'normal' release date. Others may practise a measured degree of intransigence towards the authorities as a way of maintaining a sense of independence – see the notes above on how Kershaw was handling his sentence. Belligerence and intransigence are not characteristic of lifers, however.

Goffman's fourth style is 'conversion', where the inmate comes to give up his own values and adopt those of the staff. In concentration camps, for example, Bettelheim describes 'Kapos', who were inmates promoted to a position of authority over other inmates: typically these expressed personal contempt for inmates and behaved even more brutally towards them than did the regular camp guards. Prefects in boarding schools often adopt this style, acting *and thinking* like members of staff in their dealings with other pupils. In mental hospitals patients sometimes adopt a 'paramedical auxiliary' role, acting as though they were nurses or even doctors by caring for patients, 'keeping them in line' and even offering medical or psychiatric advice; the same is common with long-stay ambulant patients in 'ordinary' hospitals. There were one or two such cases among the lifers – prisoners who became 'tea boys' and the like and appeared to some extent to adopt prison officers' attitudes towards other prisoners – but this was extremely rare.

There were more cases of what one might call 'agreement' rather than 'conversion' – adoption of staff values rather than staff behaviour, or even being in the position of already holding these values rather than having acquired them from the staff – and using the institution as an instrument for achieving its and your own agreed purpose. This is a common orientation in sixth forms and universities – the aim of 'acquiring an education' is the chosen aim of the students as well as of the institution. Despite Goffman's suggestions to the contrary, it would also appear to be a common orientation in mental hospitals. Caudill *et al* (1952), for instance, in their ward observation study, suggest that by far the most frequent response from other patients to those who found the restrictions of the institution galling was that they were there to cooperate in a cure and that it was against their own interests to 'fight' the doctors. I noticed an element of this 'agreement' in many of the interviews with lifers; prisoners themselves posited that there must be something wrong with them, to explain the offence which they had committed, and looked to the prison system to provide treatment facilities. This was most common, as one might expect, among men whose murder involved a sexual element.

Furthermore, 'conversion' might fruitfully be seen as an example of a much more general phenomenon which I am tempted to call 'escape'. What happens is that the inmate, after a considerable search (or perhaps even fortuitously), finds a role which can be played in the institution but yet is respectable in its own right, both in the sense that other people can respect it and that he can respect himself because of it. It may be a role imported from the outside world. Doctors in the army continue to be doctors in prisoner of war camps. Bettelheim's own way of surviving the concentration camps was to continue, as a psychologist, to do research into how people around him were surviving them. A woman who comes into prison pregnant or with a very young child can hardly be said to be in prison at all, except for the inconvenience; the role and duties of motherhood take up most of her time and energies (see Ward, 1973). Some married men in prison – some of the lifers in my sample – go through the prison day mechanically, saving all their spare time and mental energies for keeping in touch with their families, writing letters, making models and toys for the children, and remain husbands and fathers who happen to be in prison rather than prisoners who happen to be married. Others find a new role in prison. The role of staff orderly, or of 'someone who looks after mental patients' is respectable.

So is the role of student. The prison in which the lifer sample lived had very good educational facilities, including provision for Open University degrees and diplomas in graphic art and design, and several of the lifers had become full-time students or artists: not only on full-time education during the day but also giving much of their spare time to it and on occasion working through the night in order to finish something. They were rarely seen in the normal associational activities of prisoners, because they could not spare the time for them. Others became full-time skilled tradesmen – there was a mechanic and a plumber in the sample, both of whom learned their trade in prison; they were on call in the way that a plumber might be on call in the outside world and took a craftsman's pride in their work. 'Gleaning' as discussed by Irwin (1970) – the use of prison facilities and programmes to change one's lifestyle or future opportunities – includes activities related to this style; while some inmates may use the programmes simply because they happen to be there, as a means of passing time, others throw themselves whole-heartedly into study or therapy and thereby give themselves a means of being different from other prisoners and enhancing their self-esteem. Educational facilities are most often used in this way in men's prisons, but it would appear that even tradi-tional prison activities such as dealing with contraband goods can have this function; the 'merchant' activities outlined by Sykes (1958) and analysed in detail by Williams and Fish (1974) are sufficiently like those of a 'hustler' outside that there may be a considerable continuity of role. A similar continuity is mentioned by Delavignette (1950), writing about French West Africa: '. . . there are some Africans who, if you put them in prison, would become a sort of domestic servant and end by regarding themselves as members of your family.' (p. 86)

One of the 'hard-core' men's solution to the problems of imprisonment was an unexpected and sweeping one: sur-rounded by men and deprived of status and opportunity, he 'became a woman'. 'Edward Guildford' (known as 'Clara' to staff and prisoners and to himself) came into prison in his mid-twenties after committing a sexual assault on a child; he was married but separated from his wife, who divorced him after conviction. As a sex offender he received the usual adverse attention of other prisoners. In his second year he suddenly declared to medical staff that he had been a transvestite for as long as he could remember, that he wished to be a woman and that he would not leave prison except as a woman. During the next seven years he made several attempts at self-castration (one nearly successful), and a visiting psychotherapist recom-mended a sex-change operation; this was not permitted by the authorities, but he was permitted to take hormone therapy and he developed breasts. Much of his relationship to prison and the prison authorities since that time has been dominated by his or her attempts to establish and reinforce a feminine role: for example, she rejects factory labour as unfeminine, preferring kitchen work and other domestic duties. Early in sentence she had shunned company but in mid-sentence she came to use her sexuality as a weapon against those who had persecuted her in the past. Now, she would claim, she has settled down to a steady – and rarely physical – relationship with two or three boyfriends. She has more or less broken off contact with her family and intends that contact shall cease altogether before her release but would claim to have ex-prisoner boyfriends outside to whom she could go after relase.

The story of Clara is a very clear illustration of how it is possible to reconstruct life 'in the mind', to change the nature of the environment without altering its physical nature. Clara did not change the structure of the prison, or the nature of prison work, or the nature of the sentence she was serving. (Indeed, she well knew she risked increasing the term she served, by coming adversely to official notice.) What she did change was her own mental construction of these circumstances and her own gender, first mentally and behaviourally and then to an extent physically. This in turn, after initial resistance, changed the way others viewed her and behaved towards her; prisoners who know her, and even some of the staff, now treat her as a woman rather than a homosexual. (She certainly impressed me with her femininity in interview.) Much the same is true of the students or the craftsmen who practised this style: they changed first themselves, then the reactions of others to them, and thence the prison world. Clara's case stands out from the others, however, because unlike them she had no official encourage-ment for her change of role but forced it through against official opposition.

Of major importance for social psychology here is the volun-taristic implication that this style of coping has for construct theory. The broad Kellian perspective that we know the world through active construing – that we see and understand the world only by imposing a 'theory' or 'world picture' on it – can often leave the *source* of this world picture unclear. It is possible to write a deterministic version of construct theory, contrary as it would be to Kelly's intention, in which constructs are modified mechanically in response to environmental feedback without any implication of an active person performing the modification; one can imagine a 'construing machine'. Cases such as Clara's, or the students, or the craftsman's, would not fit such a deterministic model. Here what we have is people who have set out deliberately to reconstrue the social world and have succeeded in changing it. The process is of course an interactive one, involving the people around the actor as well as the actor himself – the role is reinforced and, ultimately, made possible by the fact that others are prepared to accept it. In the case of the students or the craftsmen the process may even have been other-initiated: it may have been prison staff who first directed the prisoners to these outlets for their energies and subsequently encouraged them in them. In Clara's case, however, the reconstruction was definitely initiated by Clara. She had some help along the way – particularly from a visiting psychotherapist – but the difficult first stages were carried through without help and in the teeth of official opposition and the scorn of other prisoners.

New roles are, of course, adopted not by meditation or mental change but by taking them on actively and playing them. To 'be a student', one studies. In the case of Open University students there are course units (printed teaching texts) to be read, plus other set or recommended reading to which the student is directed, weekly or monthly tutorials (run in prison by a visiting tutor) to be attended, television programmes to be watched, radio programmes to listen to, essays or other assignments to be posted off at regular intervals, and an examination at the end of the year for which preparation has to be made. Open University students in the outside world have to sit down each week and plan a timetable for the week's work of from five to twenty hours of study (on average), depending on the number of courses taken simultaneously. The student who is a prisoner also has this to do, and it is a procedure with two advantages for him: the study timetable fills his empty hours, and each adherence to the timetable reaffirms for him the fact that he is a student. Similarly, the 'woman' who is a prisoner builds a routine – a time to do the housework, a time to sew, a time to wash the hair, a time to apply cosmetics – and this routine segments time and reaffirms her femininity. One notices an element of stereotyping in the way the role is played: the students are conscious of themselves as students, the woman is self-consciously female, and all the routine elements of the role tend to have that extra quality of deliberation and perfectionism, often lacking in students or women who are just 'in' a role rather than 'playing' one. One is reminded to an extent of the anecdote about the sisters who 'played being sisters'; the enactment of the role is always a performance, with little off-stage relaxation about it. Nonetheless, paradoxically, it does restore the separation of 'spheres of life' which is so conspicuously absent in total institutions. The student, for example, has times when he is free to be a student and other times when he is forced to be just a prisoner, and this may divide life up in ways akin to the normal separation of home life, working life, trips to the local pub and so on. As well as a long-term calendar and short-term timetable, the adopted role may well increase the 'density' of daily life and give it a more varied texture.

Although strong parallels may be drawn with how we all cope with the outside world, there are two important differences. First, in the outside world there is a 'prime reality' which for most of us has a certain solidity and functions as a return point from our doubts about our identity:

> This is the reality of everyday life. Its privileged position entitles it to the designations of paramount reality. . . . [it] imposes itself upon consciousness in the most massive, urgent and intense manner. It is impossible to ignore, difficult even to weaken in its imperative presence. (Berger and Luckman, 1972, p. 35)

The 'escape' identity to which some of us may on occasions resort is often an escape *from* this prime or paramount reality: we may, 'go there' in order to simplify a life which is becoming unduly complex or over-burdened with routine invitations to submerge our identity. For the prisoner the opposite is generally the case, because the 'paramount reality' of prison is thin, drab and empty of events.

> There is a density to everyday consciousness which at most times gives us a sense that 'life is going along' . . . There may be moments when we look around and wonder where we are or what we are doing but we soon pick up the threads again and get back to the rich fabric of life. . . . we do not typically see our own life as a mere succession of discrete events, we recognise that our activities . . . are fastened firmly to a set of structured ideas.   (Cohen and Taylor, 1976, pp. 17–18)

The 'escape' of the lifer is an escape *into* this rich fabric, to try to find a set of structured ideas which will allow a meaningful existence.

Secondly, we must note that progress in the new career identity may be blocked, or at least rendered extremely difficult, by arbitrary action of the system. What happens to the student who is suddenly moved to another prison where Open University facilities are not made available? Does he maintain the student identity or does it fade? What happens to a student ten years after sentence who has achieved his degree and still has no promise of a release date? Again, does the identity fade and the protection it conveyed become nullified? In Chapter 3 it was noted, without much comment, that interest in classes and courses as a way of getting through sentence is one of the characteristics which declines between men in the main run of sentence and men in the 'hard-core' sample. How many harrowing failures to maintain a student self-identity could be concealed in that simple measurement, one wonders? (The only case I know at first hand is a hopeful one; he finished his degree, started an Open University higher degree while in prison and was still continuing after release when I last met him. The questions remain, however.)

4.4:   *Provision of identity*

So far the tone of this chapter has been strongly voluntaristic, stressing the deliberate adoption of 'styles' or 'identities' through which to cope with prison life at an advantage. Two questions remain for us to consider, at least in brief outline. First, where do these identities come from? Secondly, what are we to say about the majority of prisoners, acknowledged in the last section, who cannot be said to adopt a style of identity but rather just cope from day to day, 'keeping their noses clean' and waiting for release?

On the second question, I am inclined to say that all prisoners adopt an identity on entering prison or early in sentence – the identity of 'the prisoner'. This is not a protective identity such as that of a student or craftsman; even prisoners despise and hold in low esteem the role of the prisoner (see, for example, Heskin *et al*, 1974; Chang *et al*, 1975; Chang and Zastrow, 1976). However, it is an identity in the sense that it consists of a coherent set of rules for how to behave, react and feel about prison events which the prisoner can take on and use to reduce uncertainty. Flanagan (1981) describes a 'long-term prisoner perspective' whose components are care in the forming and conduct of relationships to 'maintain face' and to respect the other, care to take only considered action and consider all options, and a knowledge of the system and its possibilities and limitations of action; behavioural correlates are the avoidance of trouble and the desire to *use* time to advantage rather than just letting it pass. This kind of perspective would seem to me fairly compatible with the stance adopted by the more settled of the lifers to whom I spoke. It seems reasonable to assume that this perspective is learned in prison; as I said earlier, lifers do not lack advice on how to 'do' their sentence. Furthermore:

> Other long termers provide information and act as a filtering agent. Elements of the perspective are passed on through pre-scriptions concerning 'right' behaviour as well as through the articulation of attitudes and opinions on issues. (Flanagan, 1981, p. 215)

Over and above this kind of specifically 'long-termer' adaptation, however, there is a general though vague understanding of how prisoners are to behave – an understanding of their subordinate position, their lack of ownership in time and property, the abrogation of rights, and so on. This would appear to be 'provided by the culture' rather than learned in prison; prisoners bring it into prison with them, even in they have not been 'inside' before. In Zimbardo's 'simulated prison experiment' (Zimbardo, 1972, 1973; Haney *et al*, 1973), perfectly ordinary American college students were arbitrarily allocated to be guards or prisoners and 'sent to prison' in a basement in Stanford University. The 'prisoners' became more distressed than is typical of actual prisoners – to the extent where the experiment had to be terminated ahead of schedule – but this may be because they had no established prisoners from whom to take advice and example on how to deal with the situation. In a 'prison' with no history or established routine, however, never having been in prison, watched over by guards with no experience of prison, they nonetheless behaved like prisoners. At one point a delegation of prisoners – who were paid volunteers free to leave at any time – came to Zimbardo as 'governor' and 'asked for parole'; they were prepared to forfeit their earnings if he would let them go. When he denied their request, they returned meekly to their cells. Concealed recorders revealed that when the prisoners were away from open observation they did not talk about their 'real' lives as students, but almost exclusively about prison matters. In general their behaviours and attitudes were judged by an experienced prison chaplain to be those of typical 'first-offender' prisoners. Thus it would appear that rule-following, respect for authority, elision of rights and a narrowing of attention to the immediate circumstances must be built into our culture's stereotype of what one should do as a prisoner.

Possibly what we are talking about here is not so much an

identity as a set of 'norms' or 'expectations' – definitions of the situation and how to behave in it. These 'sets' abound in any culture and may be distinguished conceptually from the 'role-prescriptions' with which they are associated. Thus for example in studying family life one is well aware of the roles of mother and father, husband and wife, but often less aware of the underlying norms which define the family as an institution and a situation for its members. Often it takes a contrast with the abnormal to cast light on the normal and taken for granted. Studying families one of whose children is labelled as educationally subnormal, for example, I was struck by the fact that we *applaud* parent's decisions to rear a mentally handicapped child themselves rather than commit him or her to an institution but *take for granted* the similar decision of parents whose children are 'normal'. More precisely, no such decision is taken in the latter case; it is just taken for granted by the parents and everyone around them that parents bring up children – this is what 'being in a family' *means*. We have, not so much *rules* for behaviour in such situations but rather 'automatic' *perceptions* of what is done there. These are absorbed via parents, peers and the media from the surrounding culture, which might be seen for this purpose as the body of historically and structurally influenced shared expectations which enables us to classify and act in situations – the shared constructs, to use Kelly's term – and thereby determine the larger part of our understanding and our behaviour. It would appear that there is at least a rudimentary set of norms in our culture even for such 'non-identities' as that of the prisoner.

Among the two sets of positive identities which our culture provides – those that are available to form the basis of an 'escape' in the sense of the last section – the lesser set comprises those which are assigned to women. While many (perhaps most) women have a work identity nowadays, there are still many whose pride and self-image is bound up in the rearing of children and this provides a positive form of identity. Women whose work means that family may have to take second place in the timetable on occasions may feel guilt for this reason and express a wish amounting to the awareness of an obligation that they could devote themselves more to the children (see Edgell, 1980). The other major role which is available, 'housewife', is not a positive identity but a negative one; it translates as 'woman who has chosen not to work'.

There is a respectable variant, however, which is half-jokingly called 'lady of leisure' by those who assume it: the married woman whose children have reached school age, so that in return for running the household she is free to undertake unpaid charitable work or social activities. The 'model' for this role, I suspect, is the life of a middle-class, middle-aged woman of the last generation who lived in a small (possibly rural) community and was a mainstay of 'Meals on Wheels', the Womens Voluntary Service or the parish organization. In preliminary analysis (Abbott and Sapsford, 1983) of our work on mothers of the mentally handicapped – which can be another sort of life sentence situation – it soon became apparent that most 'just coped' with parenthood, to varying degrees, but that a few had classified their situation as that of permanent child-rearer or of 'lady of leisure' (two of them using that phrase) and used this identity as a way of coming to terms with the problem. For male prisoners no equivalent of these identities appears to be available, unless we wish to stretch a metaphor and regard Goffman's 'colonists' as the equivalent of 'ladies of leisure', making a hope within a provided situation and turning its deprivations into perceived advantages. (In women's prisons, however, there are reported attempts at building family relationships as a form of adaptation – see, e.g., Ward and Kassebaum, 1971.)

Our culture's dominant prestigious identities, largely reserved still for males in the cultural stereotype, are all to do with the area of work. Prison is a form of unemployment for men – work identities are stripped away and the responsibility to have a job or career; what is called *work* in prison is actually more akin to occupational therapy, a set of activities provided by the authorities to help pass the hours of the day. The deprivation of timetables and careers which real work provides can be a devastating experience, even for those who did not have a 'career job' in the outside world:

> Anyone who knows how tenaciously the working class has fought for more leisure . . . might think that even among the misery of unemployment, men would still benefit from having unlimited free time. On examination this leisure proves to be a tragic gift. Cut off from their work and deprived of contact with the outside world, the workers of Marienthal have lost the material and moral incentive to make use of their time. Now that they are no longer under any pressure, they undertake nothing new and drift gradually out of an ordered existence into one that is undisciplined and empty. Looking back over any

period of their free time, they are unable to recall anything worth mentioning . . .   (Jahoda *et al*, 1972, p. 66)

Worse in many ways, however, is the loss of status, the loss of any marker by which to locate oneself within the social world:

> . . . social status and personal identity are closely intertwined . . . people tend to accept [their work] as one clear element in defining themselves to themselves and are reluctant to dispense with this support for their personal identity. In [Jahoda's study of unemployment in Marienthal] the unemployed were asked on their time budget sheets to state their occupation. Those between twenty one and fifty tended to identify themselves as 'unemployed'. This adaptation in the middle years to unemployment as a status and self-definition and thereby to being outsiders to normal social life, is evidence for the social disintegration that went in that community with long term unemployment.   (Jahoda, 1982, p. 26)

It is perhaps encouraging that the men I interviewed used the term 'prisoner' frequently to describe others, particularly in tones of contempt, but never to describe themselves as individuals. Its only self-directed use was in the plural, as a collective to distinguish 'prisoners' from, for example, 'prison officers'.

Given the pressing need for a 'work identity' for males in our culture and the equivalence in status of imprisonment and unemployment, it is not remarkable that the 'escape' identities which we have identified are all work identities. The key ones which I have described are 'student' and 'craftsman', both usually prestigious in working-class company as respectively a step out of one class into potentially the higher reaches of another and the summit of achievement within the class. Other roles which have been adopted include that of 'artist' – the man described in section 4.2 who has worked his way through different arts and crafts in 'two-year plans' – and 'song writer'. Where a true work identity is not chosen, a pastime of the status of work may take its place – one of the 'hard core', for example, thought of himself for a long time as a potential amateur boxing champion.

The exception, on the face of it, is Clara, who has opted for the role of woman. I would argue, however, that Clara does not play a role which a woman would select for herself under similar circumstances. He is not planning to raise a family – to bear his own children is a physical impossibility and his record precludes adoption. He has no taste for prison's opportunities for a 'lady of leisure'. He is not a 'career girl', not even a 'prostitute' now. (The height of his aspiration is 'housewife', perhaps, to look after some boyfriend's house – a female role, but not a high-status one.) Moreover, the way he goes about being a woman is not a woman's way: women of his age do not demand feminine work, nor practise make-up as a hobby activity to a time schedule. One cannot so easily escape one's cultural conditioning: Clara, it can be argued, is 'being a woman' after the fashion of a man – he has made a job out of it.

My point is that voluntarism has its limits. There is a 'resting-level reality' which broadly constrains what we are free to do. We see the broad lines of our reality through the constructs which our culture provides. We are free, if structural circumstances permit or can be 'twisted' to permit it, to be lawyers or students or plumbers but not Samurai, because we do not know what it is to be Samurai; at most we could be English imitations of Samurai. Similarly, when a man tries to be a woman, he is overwhelmingly likely to become a man's conception of a woman rather than a woman's.

However, within that balance of probabilities the choice and the construction are still our own; identities are not forced *on* us, but adopted *by* us. Several cases have been discussed of men who have 'changed identity' as sentence progressed, some of them assuredly on the rational – though not necessarily articulated – assessment that change was needed if he were ever to get out of prison. Others (for example, Kershaw) persist in their chosen style of moderate non-cooperation despite an explicit realization in Kershaw's case that he was 'cutting off his nose to spite his face'. It is difficult not to use the word 'choice' under these circumstances.

5

TOWARDS A CRITICAL
PSYCHOLOGY

5.1: *Summary: the history of a project's interpretation*

In the book so far the 'story' of what it is like to be a life-sentence prisoner has been told and retold around the three themes or organizing concepts of reaction, response and change. We have looked at predicted 'reactions' to prison as a temporally extended stimulus-configuration, at prisoners' actions ('responses' in the sense that one 'responds' to a conversational remark) in reply to the deprivation of key aspects of normal life which the life sentence enforces on them, and at the 'changes' which some prisoners are able to impose on prison life by the way that they have come to construe their place within it (or sometimes, effectively *outside* it). This last chapter has a different purpose, to look inwards at the nature of social psychology as a distinctive intellectual endeavour. First, however, let us summarize briefly what has gone before and set it in the context of broader psychological theory.

Chapter 3 set out the original conception of this research in 1975 when the fieldwork was carried out, as a contribution to a branch of social learning theory. A model was constructed of human reaction to situations in which the hypothesized 'core self-concept' of one's capabilities and one's place in the world is destroyed or put under threat, drawing heavily on the 'learned helplessness' work of Martin Seligman and his colleagues, and predictions were made from it about how prisoners serving life sentences should react to their imprisonment. Empirical study of sixty life-sentence prisoners failed to confirm these predictions. The initial phase of anxiety and disorientation which was predicted did indeed appear to occur, but there was little or no evidence of a subsequent lapse into depression, dependence, withdrawal and/or apathy which was expected as a reaction to the growing certainty that one's life course was beyond one's control. On the contrary, prison life appeared despite its undisputed drabness and lack of stimulation to provide limited but sufficient scope for the assertion of personal control. It was argued as a *'post hoc* rationalization' that the theory was not necessarily invalidated: rather, the nature of the environment may not have been as was supposed.

Chapter 4 rejected the deterministic 'model of man' underlying this kind of theorizing – organism acting on and acted on by environment, with 'person' just a conventional term for the *mechanisms* linking environmental stimulus to behavioural reaction – and attempted an account which would treat persons more as *people*. That is, the story which Chapter 4 tells is a story about intelligent self-direction, about responding to or replying to the environment by taking action to change it. We looked at how prisoners come to terms with the fact of their offence and the fact of being in prison on an indeterminate sentence – the 'dialogue' which they conduct with others and with themselves about the kind of people they are and the kind of future they may expect. We looked at how people construct or discover 'landmarks' and 'events' to provide a tolerable structuring of indeterminate time. At a more concrete level of action, we saw how people recreate the possibility of personal space and personal property in an environment where these two key features of 'ordinary life' are supposed to be absent. We looked also at long-term 'career plans' – what the prisoner may *do* about prison life as a whole. The approach of the earlier sections of Chapter 4 might be seen as akin to action research – making a change in the environment and seeing what people do about it – except that the 'change' was instituted by the courts rather than the researcher. (Alternatively, what the *prisoners* do about their lives might be seen as action research – 'man the scientist' taking actions and assessing their personal consequences.) The underlying 'paradigm' of the chapter is that of Kelly (1955) or Rogers (1951), or the powerful restatement in the collection edited by Reason and Rowan (1981): the notion that 'research subjects' are people like us, and that we can relevantly use the same criteria for assessing their actions and motives that we use for assessing our own. In the terms used by John Shotter (1974), the chapter deals with 'reasons', not 'causes'.

Fundamental to the perspectives of Kelly or Rogers, how-ever, is the proposition that we can only act on the world as we see it and understand it – that the world is something of which we *make* sense. Chapter 4 moved away from a straightforward 'action perspective' to a more fundamentally Kellian analysis of how prisoners construe their world and their future – what sense they are able to make of it. Using a reworked version of Goffman's typology of responses to the total institution, it looked at the few prisoners who cannot make sense of the environment at all except by effectively withdrawing from both past and future, at the equally small number who come to see prison as home, at those who adopt the authorities' perspective towards their 'case' (or more often, who already shared that perspective and are using the facilities to effect their own 'cure') and at those who are able to reconstruct prison life by finding a respectable role within it. At one level, it was argued, this is the majority response: most prisoners act the role of prisoner 'according to the rules of the role' and thereby acquire a structure within which to act. More interesting, however, were the few cases where what occurred was not so much *construing* as *constructing*: the prison world was 'understood' by turning it into something else in the case of some 'students' or 'tradesmen', or by changing oneself into something else in Clara's case. (Clara's case was particularly important for this essentially voluntaristic analysis because she was not using facilities provided by the authorities to impose new meaning on the situation, but rather forcing through a change of meaning against institutional pressure.)

The perspectives adopted in Chapter 4 mostly have a strongly voluntaristic implication – they suggest that the indi-vidual is entirely free to act in response to circumstances and fairly free to 'change the world' by changing the way in which he chooses to regard it. Such apparent undue voluntarism is a common fault in psychological writing of the humanistic, con-structivist variety. Kelly himself often writes as though we can have untrammelled freedom to change our constructs (the categories by which we make sense of the world) and is dis-cretely vague about constructs' origins. However, constructs most logically come from *somewhere*, and the later part of Chapter 4 gives a brief and superficial account of the possible origins of how we see the world and thus of the constraints which set the boundaries of intelligent self-determination. The chapter does not deal with the personal origins of constraint –

developmental factors such as are explored in the work of Freud, Erikson and their many successors, or acquired habits of judgement and behaviour such as are the stock-in-trade of learning theory. Nor does it explore the explicit effects of structure on life-space, because these are less problematic in prison than in most other social locations: the physical and social constraints of imprisonment are all too obvious. What the chapter does begin to explore is the repertoire of 'roles' which our culture makes available – the ways of assigning meaning, structure and purpose to our activities which are easily adopt-able within our society and provide at least an outline template within which we can construct a personalized life. It is sug-gested that the range of 'personalized lives' which it is possible for the person to construct easily is severely limited by what has developed historically within his or her culture, and that the 'cultural repertoire' in turn is heavily influenced by structural and economic factors. Drawing on the work from Fromm (e.g. 1976) and on Marxist and feminist sociologists, I have sug-gested that most (or all?) 'respectable' roles in our culture centre around the areas of work and profession or motherhood and home-making – the latter being seen as the inferior set of the two – and that the convenience of this concentration for an industrial and capitalistic form of economic organization is hardly coincidental.

Thus the movement within these two chapters is from volun-tarism back to determinism – from freedom of action to con-straint in our 'perception' of the meaning of circumstances and the meaningful alternative available for dealing with them. I would wish to make the move a dialectical one, however, and to assert that the deterministic elements at the end of Chapter 4 are different in kind from the determinism of Chapter 3. I would not wish to deny that developmental factors and the accidents of stimulus–response learning can shape our behaviour and our understanding without our knowing it. I have positively as-serted that cultural and, ultimately, structural factors put a hedge around what it seems natural for us to do and to be in any given circumstance and that they may often rule out certain courses of action by determining what we 'take for granted' as being the natural order of things. Such factors predispose the unaware subject towards certain courses and styles of action, but once he or she becomes aware of them they lose much of their determining force. If I know that I am afraid of certain situations, then the possibility exists that I can overcome my fear. If I detect an automatic pattern in my response to people, then the possibility exists that I can respond differently on different occasions. If taken-for-granted factors can be made explicit in consciousness, then like Clara's gender they may prove less than immutable. The final 'metatheoretical position' of this book, therefore, is one of self-determination within constraint which emphasizes the crucial role of awareness as a facilitator of change and of social psychology as a tool for promoting awareness.

5.2: *Psychology as science fiction*

The 'paradigm' of Chapter 3 treated social psychology very much as a social *science*, and what was to be expected from the interaction of theory and data was clear: predictions were made on the basis of theory and these predictions were tested against measurements abstracted from the lifer data. In Chapter 4, however, a different kind of paradigm is invoked, for a different kind of purpose. Chapter 4 tries to describe 'what I have found out about lifers', but it does so by trying to express a *picture* or *image* of the lifer's existence which seems plausible and comprehensive. What is involved is a 'thought experiment' – one is trying to 'tell the story' of what it must be like to live the lives of the research informants, based on the interviews and reports which had been collected and my experience of hanging around prisons for several years talking to people.

Thinking about this kind of approach to social psychology, it has seemed to me that there are parallels with what some writers of science fiction are trying to do for their audiences: there is this same element of 'telling a story' in order to illuminate our own lives. One of my favourite novels, for example, is Ursula LeGuin's *The Left Hand of Darkness*, which describes the experiences of a 'normal' envoy sent as 'first contact' to a world whose inhabitants are not bisexual but have a cyclic sexual pattern:

> For twenty-one or twenty-two days the individual is . . . sexually inactive, latent. On about the eighteenth day hormonal changes are initiated . . . and on the twenty second or twenty third day the individual enters . . . estrus. In this first phase . . . he remains completely androgynous. Gender, and potency, are not attained in isolation . . . When the individual finds a partner . . . hormonal secretation is further stimulated . . . until in one

partner either a male or female hormonal dominance is established. The genitals engorge or shrink accordingly ,. . . and the partner, triggered by the change, takes on the other sexual role . . . Normal individuals have no predisposition to either sexual role . . . they do not know whether they will be the male or female and have no choice in the matter.

At one level the plot of the novel explores the interaction of a feudal and a collectivist society neither of which has ever known capitalism. At another it traces out the consequences for social structure of a different pattern of sexuality. At another again, it is a thought experiment on the consequences of sexuality for our own self-conception. The 'normal', writing of these 'deviants', notes that:

> Our entire pattern of socio-sexual interaction is non-existent here . . . They do not see one another as men or women. This is almost impossible for our imagination to accept . . . One is respected and judged only as a human being. It is an appalling experience . . .

and again elsewhere:

> He was frank, and expected a reciprocal frankness that I might not be able to supply. He, after all, had no standards of manliness, of virility, to complicate his pride.

More insight still is given by the description written by one of the natives of how he has judged the, to him, deviant bisexual:

> There is a frailty about him. He is all unprotected, exposed, vulnerable, even to his sexual organ which he must carry always outside himself; but he is strong, unbelievably strong . . . To match his frailty and strength, he has a spirit easy to despair . . . a fierce impatient, courage. This slow, hard, crawling work we have been doing these days wears him out in body and will, so that if he were one of my race I should think him a coward, but he is anything but that; he has a ready bravery I have never seen the like of. He is ready, eager, to stake life on the cruel quick test.

What we have here is one consequence of human sexuality as seen from outside, insofar as it is ever possible for us to see ourselves from outside. (LeGuin does in fact see virility from outside, as she is a woman.) A 'model of man' is built up and displayed and we learn about ourselves by studying it. LeGuin is in one sense a social psychologist and of the newer variety; in Shotter's words (1975, p. 14) she seeks understanding:

so that by understanding more clearly what we are and the situation or 'position' we occupy, we may be able to describe explicitly the possibilities available to us all for what we might do next, for what we might make of ourselves and our world.

One would certainly be hard pressed to divide her, on these criteria, from Watson or Skinner or Freud or Rogers, all of whom are explicitly engaged in understanding the nature of man in order to change the world; she builds a model of what it is like to be human which is quite as compelling as the ones which they have purveyed.

In the 1930 revised edition of *Behaviourism*, Watson sets out the 'plot' or essential idea of that branch of psychology very clearly:

> Behaviourism . . . was an attempt to do one thing – to apply to the experimental study of man the same kind of procedure and the same language that many research men had found useful in the study of animals lower than man. We believed . . . that man is an animal different from other animals only in the type of behaviour he displays . . . The raw fact (is) that you, as a psychologist, if you are to remain scientific, must describe the behaviour of man in no other terms than those you would use in describing the behaviour of the ox you slaughter.

This is very much a science-fiction endeavour, to try out the implications of explaining all human behaviour in the terms developed by learning theorists, and Watson gives the idea a very fair run for its money. Of conscious experience, for example, he writes that: '. . . belief in the existence of consciousness goes back to the ancient days of superstition and magic . . .' and he characterizes thinking as: 'language habits – habits which when exercised implicitly behind the closed doors of the lips we call thinking.' Social relations are characterized in a very similar way:

> . . . shortly afterwards, the two men became friends and saw one another every day and became really acquainted – that is, formed verbal and manual habits towards one another and towards the same or similar situations.

Sometimes the impish humour of a Samuel Butler or an Oscar Wilde comes through, as when he suggests that:

> It is obvious that humans stop learning too soon. Something ought to be done to disturb the average householder once in a while and force him to learn something new.

Or when he parodies his own language game:

> Since the advent of the conditioned reflex hypothesis in psychol-
> ogy . . . I have had my own larygeal processes stimulated to
> work upon this problem from another angle.

One can never be sure, however, just when Watson is over-
emphasizing for humorous effect and when he wishes to be
taken entirely seriously. Some of his practical suggestions are
outrageous beyond the bounds of humour. Of the treatment of
the mentally ill, for example, he writes that: 'The question as to
whether the hopelessly insane should be etherised has of course
been raised time and time again. There can be no reasons
against it except exaggerated sentiment and mediaeval religi-
ous mandates' and in his own practical research he is perfectly
prepared to carry out his experiments on institutionalized
children. He becomes positively querulous about the Hecksher
Foundation, for example, where he and Mary Jones carried out
numerous manipulations of the behaviour of young children: 'It
was not an ideal place for our experimental work because we
were not allowed full control of the children.'
For another prolific writer of this kind of science fiction, and
one who badly shocked his first audience, we might go to
Vienna in the early years of the century, to the works of
Sigmund Freud. One of his stories, for example, puts forward a
picture of what it is like to be a child quite unlike the then
generally accepted one:

> The little boy may show the most undisguised sexual curiosity
> about his mother, he may insist on sleeping beside her at night,
> he may force his presence on her while she is dressing or may
> even make actual attempts at seducing her, as his mother will
> often notice and report with amusement . . . A human being's
> first choice of an object is regularly an incestuous one . . .
> (Freud, 1917)

He even has a good reason to offer why this account should
seem so new and shocking to his audience:

> So far as I know, not a single author has clearly recognised the
> regular existence of a sexual instinct in childhood . . . The reason
> for this strange neglect is to be sought, I think, partly in con-
> siderations of property . . . (but) . . . partly in a psychological
> phenomenon which has itself hitherto eluded explanation.
> What I have in mind is the peculiar *amnesia* which, in the case of
> most people, hides the earliest beginnings of their childhood up

to their sixth or eighth year . . . (and) turns everyone's childhood into something like a *prehistoric* epoch and conceals from him the beginnings of his own sexual life.   (Freud, 1905)

Another of his plots describes a race (the human one) in which much of the basic tendency of behaviour in the developing individual can be described by the two factors of hedonism and respect for reality:

> The sexual instincts, from beginning to end of their develop-
> ment, work towards obtaining pleasure; they retain their origi-
> nal function unaltered. The other instincts, the ego-instincts,
> have the same aim to start with. But under the influence of the
> instructuress Necessity . . . (they discover) that it is inevitable
> for (them) to renounce immediate satisfaction . . . (and to obey)
> to the reality principle, which also at bottom seeks to obtain
> pleasure, but pleasure which is assured though taking account
> of reality . . . This transition from the pleasure principle to the
> reality principle is one of the most important steps forward in
> the ego's development.   (Freud, 1917)

To liken Freud or Skinner or Watson to science fiction writers would cause litle surprise among those who profess themselves opposed to one or the other school (or both). I maintain, however, that *all* psychological writing shares much with science fiction, because all psychology purveys a model of man. Skinner has man entirely determined by environment and Freud stresses the crucial importance of early learning and experience (though with some ambiguity in his determinism), but both share the image of man as machine – 'a complicated, going, organic machine', to use Watson's words. Some deter-minists say that what we do is the result of our biological constitution (the machine's 'hardware'), some that early learn-ing (the programmed software) is the determinant and some that immediate environment (the input) is crucial, but for none of them is there anything corresponding to the ordinary-language concept 'person'. They all, effectively, say, 'Let us imagine a world in which all behaviour is determined, in a machine-like way, by biology or by environment', which is a good science fiction idea. Rogers or Shotter (or I) would say 'Imagine instead a world where people can determine their own actions within constraints', an equally science fiction concept though leading perhaps to a less outlandish and caricatured plot line. We are all inviting the reader to enter an imaginary world, in order to cast light on his or her own.

The world which Carl Rogers (1951) invites us to accept as
our own, for instance, is one which is defined by as many science
fiction concepts as the one which the Behaviourists construct,
but with a greater likelihood of the story leading to a happy
ending. He starts from the proposition that we all live in private
worlds:

> Every individual exists in a continually changing world of
> experience of which he is the centre . . . An important truth in
> regard to this . . . world . . . is that it can only be known, in any
> genuine or complete sense, to the individual himself . . . I can
> never know with vividness or completeness how a pinprick or a
> failure in an examination is experienced by you. The world of
> experience is for each individual, in a very significant sense, a
> private world.
>
> This complete and first hand acquaintance with the world of
> his total experience is . . . only potential . . . my actual awareness
> of and knowledge of my total phenomenal field is limited. It is
> still true, however, that potentially I am the only one who can
> know it in its completeness.

This leads to the concept of multiple individual realities,
checked by comparison but in no sense absolute:

> The organism reacts to the field as it is experienced
> and perceived. This perceptual field is, for the individual, 'real-
> ity' . . . While it is not necessary for our own purposes to define
> any absolute concept of reality, it should be noted that we are
> continually checking our perceptions against one another . . .
> Thus the world comes to be composed of a series of tested
> hypotheses which provide much security. Yet mingled with
> these . . . are perceptions which remain completely unchecked.
> These untested perceptions are also a part of our personal
> reality and may have as much authority as those which have
> been checked.

Built into the organism which Rogers is describing is a movement towards richer and more diverse perception and greater
freedom of choice and action.

> The organism has one basic tendency and striving – to
> actualise, maintain and enhance . . . Its movement . . . is in the
> direction of an increasing self-government, self-regulation and
> autonomy . . . the organic tendency towards ongoing growth
> and enhancement.

All that is needed, then, is a clearer perception of one's circumstances for one to become free:

> As I study . . . the recorded clinical cases . . . I find that the urge for a greater degree of independence, the desire for a self-determined integration, the tendency to strive, even through much pain, towards a socialised maturity . . . is stronger than the desire for comfortable dependence . . . Clinically I find it to be true that though an individual may remain dependent because he has always been so, or may drift into dependence without realising what he is doing, or may temporarily wish to be dependent because his situation appears desperate, I have yet to find the individual who, when he examines his situation deeply, and feels that he perceives it clearly, deliberately chooses . . . to have the integrated direction of himself undertaken by another. When all the elements are clearly perceived, the balance seems invariably in the direction of the painful but ultimately rewarding path of self-actualisation or growth.

Thus Rogers's theory of personality allows man the strong possibility of a happy ending.

To an extent the purveying of an image of man is a political activity, as has often been stated, because it reflects an ideology and conveys ideological propositions persuasively to the reader. The point has been well expressed by Leman (cited in Banister and Fransella, 1971):

> . . . Many scientific theories (and not least some of those contrapted by psychologists) are . . . highly significant as programmes for future events of a kind to suit the originating scientist . . . [Behaviourism, for example] doesn't really say what you are like, it says what they . . . would like you to be like; and that's fair warning that they will make you like that if they can. Everybody capable of entertaining the thought now knows that psychology is a branch of politics, mainly concerned with the disposal of bodies and the disposing of existence.

The political applications need not be sinister, however; Rogers and Shotter are also 'dispensing an existence', but one where people control their own lives, and George Kelly confesses that: 'There are, indeed, moments when I deeply suspect that man's only purpose in discovering the laws of human behaviour is to contrive some way to escape them.'   (Kelly, 1969)

Psychology has political content, certainly – everything the human does has some political content – but it seems to me that the politics of humanistic psychology is more like therapy or like science fiction: it invites the patient or the reader to imagine. 'Imagine yourself the centre of the world', says Rogers. 'Imagine a world in which you can experiment through your behaviour to test out your picture of the world', says Kelly. 'Imagine that it is possible to change the world by thinking and acting', I was saying when I described the 'escape stratagem' for coping with the life sentence. These are therapeutic state- ments in that they aim to enhance people's lives by changing their self images. They are science fiction in that they describe worlds which are often only possible, not actual for everybody; we are in the business of describing possible worlds.

There is one crucial difference, however. LeGuin says, implicitly, 'Imagine a world which is not divided into male and female; there is no such world, but imagining it may help to correct a few of the faults in the world that does exist.' I say 'Imagine that it is possible to change captivity into opportunity by reconceiving one's life.' Because psychological writing is factually based, however, I am able to go on and say more: it is not only possible, but someone has actually done so, which is a message of hope for anyone in any kind of captivity – which is all of us. Social psychology is concerned to describe and to yield understanding but also and thereby to offer the possibility of change – a sort of social therapy. In this respect, I suggest, modern social psychology shares some of the characteristics of 'critical theory' or 'critical philosophy' as the terms were used by Habermas, Adorno, Marcuse and others of the 'Frankfurt School'. The final section of this chapter and of the book is devoted to exploring this resemblance further.

5.3: *Psychology as critical theory*

Three kinds of new awareness have been growing among social psychologists during the years since the Second World War – slowly at first, and chiefly among therapists and counsellors, but at a rapidly increasing pace during the last ten years – which have found their expression in this book.

1.   It is becoming increasingly obvious that the traditional boundaries between academic disciplines have to be broken down if we are to 'make sense' of man in the modern social world. In particular social psychology has to incorporate the perspectives of a sociology which has itself already taken over a great deal from economics and politics. We are becoming

increasingly aware that the nature of the individual relates to the structure and history of macro-social relations as well as to intrapersonal developments and interpersonal interactions.

2.   Increasingly we are beginning to feel the need for a *committed* social psychology which does not regard itself as a branch of behavioural technology – and the two halves of this clause are equally important. An uncommitted, academic psychology – one which imagines that the human values of the researcher can be kept out of his or her psychology – tends all too easily to become an apologist for the existing order, elevating transitory states of experience into laws true for all times and all places. A 'behavioural technology' can too easily become the servant of the existing order and, if it is effective, hold back the very developments which its human (and therefore political) creators might wish to see occur. This is an increasing danger in a world where most spheres of life are to some extent open to official scrutiny and where a single message on television or in the popular press can reach millions of people at the same time. 'Objectivity' – excluding values from the analysis – tends to mean that social norms are also left unexamined, taken for granted. Unless we allow the examination of the taken-for-granted elements of 'human nature' at a given time and in a given society to become a core element of our analysis, social psychology has probably reached the limits of its ability to increase our understanding. Of its own nature the examination of what we generally take for granted is a critical activity and one detrimental to the existing order; it unsettles our presuppositions and weakens the force of 'social rules'. It will not be a pleasurable experience for the psychologist unless he or she is committed to improving human life as well as to understanding it.

3.   We have had borne in on us the need to be reflexive – to allow that what we study or treat or manipulate is the same kind of thing as ourselves. The social psychologist is a part of the social world, and the writings of social psychologists affect it more immediately and more dramatically for the social psychologist than for the people to whom he or she is writing. More and more we are bringing our own dissatisfactions to our psychology and expecting it to enlarge the scope of our own lives. We who 'do' social psychology as a trade or profession are increasingly coming to require that there be 'something in it for us' over and above the economic and social rewards of professional activity. (This, I remember, was what I expected of

psychology when I first studied it at university – that it would increase my understanding of myself and other people and thus make me feel more 'at home' in the adult world. Instead I was given ethology, rats, cockroaches and systems analysis of the human perceptual machinery, with the result that I turned away from the subject. My experience was by no means unique in this respect, as is demonstrated in the preface to Nigel Armistead's collection of critical essays published in 1974.)

An example of an early attempt at committed, reflexive synthesis which is still of great importance for social psychology is provided by the 'Frankfurt School', the Institute for Social Research which was founded in Frankfurt in 1923 and included among its members philosopher-sociologists such as Horkheimer and Habermas and philosopher-psychologists such as Adorno and Marcuse. A fundamental concern of this 'school' was the implication for the individual in society of the writings of Freud and Marx, and particularly the effects of social structure on individual social life, mediated as it is by a culture which they saw as reflecting the particular structure of domination and control which characterizes modern society. They characterized the approaches of writers such as Freud and Marx – and their own work – as constituting a different *kind* of scientific theory from those of the natural sciences, and they coined the term 'critical theory' to express that difference.

'Critical theories' share with those of the natural sciences the fact of being a form of knowledge – they produce statements to which the concepts of truth and falsehood may validly be applied, not just statements of aesthetic or moral preference – but they differ in being 'reflexive' rather than 'objectifying'. That is, theories in the natural sciences are a different order of 'object' from the 'things' to which they refer, but a critical theory is itself a part of the domain to which it refers. The 'objective' social world cannot be differentiated from what it means to those who are in it, and the critical theory is a part of and a contribution to that meaning. Most important, the two differ in their goals. A successful natural theory gives man control of the 'external environment', to manipulate it or to cope with it. The aim of successful critical theory is emancipation and enlightenment – making agents aware of pressures previously hidden from them and thereby *changing the nature* of the social world:

In the conviction of its founders the critical theory of society is essentially linked with materialism . . . [but] there are two basic elements linking materialism to correct social theory: concern with human happiness and the conviction that it can be attained only through a transformation of the material conditions of existence.   (Marcuse, 1937)

The transformation is to be brought about not by direct 'manipulation of the social environment', however – this would be merely to exchange one form of slavery for another – but by changing actors' awareness of the social/material context of their actions so that they themselves can take control of change. Critical theory is thus intensely voluntaristic in its goals; it wishes to bring about a change in society which will increase people's freedom of thought and action. To quote Marcuse again:

Within the institutional framework which men have given themselves in interaction with the prevailing natural and historical conditions, the development proceeds through the action of men – they are the historical agents and theirs are the alternatives and decisions.   (Marcuse, 1958, p. 12)

Here he echoes the more succinct formulation of the early Marx (1844): 'Men make history, but not in circumstances of their own choosing'. It is towards increasing the choice of circumstances that critical theory is directed.

Marcuse's work is a good example of what this kind of approach at its best can contribute to social psychology. *Eros and Civilisation* exemplifies the attempted synthesis of Marx and Freud which is one hallmark of the Frankfurt School. Marcuse takes up Freud's thesis that civilization is made possible by the repression of 'natural' sexuality from untrammelled expression and its sublimation into socially creative channels, and develops it in two directions. On the one hand, current society tends to undermine this process, using sexuality to sell the (basically unneeded) products whose production and sale has become essential to the maintenance of a capitalist distribution of power and potential; sex is linked to objects and products, used to sell instead of sublimated, and in the process its potential nature is changed and degraded. Marcuse terms this process 'repressive desublimation'. On the other hand, it is possible for the power of human sexuality to be harnessed by its possessors to build a full and unalienated style of life, provided it is not repressed arbitrarily in the interests of others:

> Under non-repressive conditions, sexuality tends to grow . . .
> towards self-sublimation in lasting and expending relations
> (including work relations) which serve to intensify and enlarge
> instinctual gratification.   (Marcuse, 1955, p. 157)

In *One-dimensional man* (1964) Marcuse looks further at the
nature of work and leisure, in a way deeply informed by the
analysis of the power of communication to control typical of
colleagues in the Frankfurt Institute such as Horkheimer and
Habermas. Marcuse points to the nature of industrial labour in
our current society as an exhausting, stupefying form of slavery,
to which typical leisure activities and the consumer commodities with which they are associated contribute by soothing
mental discomfort and prolonging the stupefaction. The 'Persil
Mum' sits happily in the midst of the consumer durables which
she and her husband have been persuaded they need by a mass
media system controlled by the establishment which sells the
goods and requires the labour. Alienated labour is powered by
media-imposed 'false' needs – serving the true interests of
those who sell, not of those who buy.

The twin themes of alienated labour and enslavement to false
needs are developed still further in the *Essay on liberation*,
published in 1969, where he preaches 'liberation . . . from the
liberties of exploitative order – a liberation which must precede
the construction of a free society' (p. 10). He emphasizes the
need for an inner liberation which must accompany changes in
material and economic circumstances if the latter are to do
more than reproduce the old society in another form:

> Each is to receive 'according to his needs' [but] what is now at
> stake are the needs themselves. At this stage, the question is no
> longer: how can the individual satisfy his own needs without
> hurting others but rather: how can he satisfy his own needs
> without hurting himself, without reproducing, through his aspir-
> ations and satisfactions, his dependence on an exploitative
> apparatus which, in satisfying his needs, perpetuates his
> servitude?

Finally, in a rare episode of 'science fiction' (in the sense of
the previous section of this chapter), he considers the possibility
of:

> . . . progress to a stage of civilisation where man has learned to
> ask for the sake of whom or what he organises his society: the
> stage where he checks and perhaps even halts his incessant

struggle for existence on an enlarged scale, surveys what has been achieved through centuries of misery and hecatombs of victims and decides that it is enough and that it is time to enjoy what he has and what can be reproduced and refined with a minimum of alienated labour.

Freedom from the rule of markets over man is seen as a precondition of any other freedom.

This kind of 'critical theory' would seem to me an important part of what we might call a 'critical psychology', but not the whole. To illuminate these 'taken-for-granted' elements of our life and experience which are in effect coercive because they serve another's interest rather than our own, and to expose the apparatus through which they are imposed, is probably the most important activity which a social psychology aimed at the enlargement and enhancement of people's lives can undertake. However, such emancipation of consciousness does not give us the material with which to work during the minutes, hours and days of everyday life. A critical psychology must also be humanistic, concerned with the quality of today's life as well as its possible future. Marcuse and his Frankfurt colleagues cast great light on human potentiality – on the world that could be – but do not help the prisoner with his captivity, the housewife with her children or the young adult with his or her need to 'establish an identity' in an established world.

Indeed, Marcuse (1937) explicitly rejects the Hegelian concept of freedom within accepted boundaries, the notion that:

> Only he is free who recognises the necessary as necessary, thereby overcoming its mere necessity . . . This is equivalent to asserting that a person born crippled who cannot be cured at the given state of medical science, overcomes this necessity when he gives reason and freedom scope within his crippled existence, i.e. if from the start he always posits his needs, goals and actions only as the needs, goals and actions of a cripple.

I would assert, however, that exactly this kind of freedom has to find a place in a critical psychology. The cripple who cannot change his crippled state still has a life to live – a life unfree because of his disability, but tending more towards freedom to the extent that he or she is aware of the fact of disability, critical of his own and other people's assumptions about what is 'proper' or 'necessary' or 'natural' in such circumstances, and aware of what others have achieved in like situations. Prisoners whose lives show features of the 'escape' stratagem discussed in Chapter 4 do not thereby think to escape *from* their captivity but they do escape *into* a style of life which offers greater productive possibilities within that captivity. The importance of one's conception of role and identity for enlarging constrained lives must not be lost in our concern to shape the future.

Several attempts to find a place for social psychology within a comprehensive critical theory have been made recently by sociologists – particularly sociologists of deviance and its relation to state control. One of the most promising for social psychology, for example, is the approach advocated by Taylor, Walton and Young in the mid-1970s in *New Criminology* and *Critical Criminology*. The full programme, laid out in *New Criminology*, sets out to provide a broad understanding of 'social phenomena' such as 'crime' by sandwiching psychology and micro-sociology between thick layers of macro-social theory. A 'fully social' explanation of criminal behaviour starts, for them, with an understanding of the social institutions which 'create' crime 'as a social category and a social problem', and the inequalities of interest which underlie these institutions – what one might call a 'political economy' of crime. Next, however, one needs to understand the people who live in this political economy – to have a *social psychology* of how people make choices and construe their collective world:

> The theory must explain the different ways in which structural demands are interpreted, reacted against or used by men at different levels in the social structure . . . a social psychology which . . . recognises that men may consciously choose the deviant road, as the one solution to the problems posed by existence in a contradictory society. (p. 271)

Next comes the study of what they call the *social dynamics* of the actual act which will come to be counted as 'criminal':

> The ways in which the actual acts of men are explicable in terms of the rationality of choice or the constraints on choice at the point of precipitation into action.

Once the act is committed, we need a social psychology or micro-sociology of social reaction and of the effects of social reaction on the deviant's further actions – a study of how the act is construed by other people (and particularly by those with the power to enforce their definitions on others), how they act in return and how the deviant reacts to the social world whose nature is changed by their responses. Finally we need to consider the wider background and origins of such reactions and the analysis tends again towards a historically informed political economy.

To a substantial extent this would appear the ideal programme for a committed, reflexive and holistic social psychology. I shall argue, however, that it is in fact the programme of a *critical sociology*, not a *critical psychology*, and that the distinction is an important one. I see three closely-linked respects in which something different is required of a critical psychology than the authors of *New Criminology* propose.

The first is a relatively trivial matter, their exclusion of *intra*personal and *infra*personal factors from the scope of social explanation:

> An adequately *social* theory would need to be free of the biological and psychological assumptions that have been involved in the various attempts to explain the actions of the men who do get defined and sanctioned by the state and react against those definitions in different historical circumstances. (p. 268)

I call this exclusion trivial because it is no way logically required or necessary for their theoretical system. One can see why workers in the field of crime might wish to react against the psychological and biological approaches which dominated criminology's early years and are still extremely influential in forensic practice. By assessing and treating a quality of 'criminality' which is seen as a property of individuals, psychological criminology has tended throughout its history to reinforce and to act as a tool of the comfortable beliefs held by those who administer the machinery of criminal justice. More important, it has tended largely to neglect the fact that 'crime' is not a behavioural category, but a socio-legal one: 'crimes' are defined by laws, which in turn reflect the balance of power and interest at a societal rather than an individual level. However, it seems unnecessary and unsatisfactory to reject altogether explanations couched at the level of the individual's biology or early socialization or environmentally programmed 'tendency to behave'. Even within criminology, the theories of someone like Eysenck about differential learning ability and psycho-biologically programmed needs to behave in certain ways are in no way incompatible with more social kinds of explanation. On the contrary, if correct they would help to explain why some individuals and not others are prone to acquire the historically and structurally important label of 'criminal'. Outside criminology, in the understanding of 'ordinary', 'everyday' living, it would be obviously foolish to neglect any insights which biology and individual psychology might be able to offer into how the unaware person can find his or her behaviour and experience constrained by a purely personal history and structure. (Many sociologists, even, are now acknowledging the importance of coming to terms with non-social kinds of explanation; see Hirst and Woolley (1982) for one particularly good adventure into this area of discourse.)

A second problem with the critical theory of *New Criminology* as a basis for a critical psychology is its specific and typically sociological concentration on 'social problems' such as crime, rather than on the whole range of human experience and potential. *New Criminology's* approach is predominantly concerned with societal, structural and historical processes – with whose interests are served by the societal world as it is, how they came to be thus served, how the current pattern is maintained as it is. It recognizes the 'world in the head' of 'personally constructed' reality and the need to look at the constraints of individuals 'at the point of precipitation into action', but only as a mediation and expression of broader structural factors which have to be understood at the level of sociology/politics/economics. Psychology thus becomes a servant of social theory rather than a full partner – useful to bridge gaps which cannot be bridged at the more societal level but not in any sense an 'initiator' of theory – and only those parts of psychology are included which can usefully serve. Those aspects of life which are not 'social problems' tend not to be problematized in this approach, and many of the naturally problematic areas of a critical social psychology (such as the nature and dynamic of everyday life) fall back into the area of the 'taken-for-granted'. A comprehensive social psychology can no more be subsumed within a 'societal' social theory than a comprehensive sociology can become a branch of social psychology, because their fundamental aims are as different as their different focuses of analysis.

This brings us to the third problem (or perhaps the third aspect of the same problem): the natural 'focus of action' of critical psychology as opposed to critical sociology. Typical of critical sociologists, the approach of Taylor, Walton and Young is concerned with social relations and rejects our natural tendency to individualize. This is the inevitable and, to my mind, salutary tendency of any sociology which takes proper account of the work of Marx and his successors: it has become obvious that one cannot account for or make sense of 'the broader social reality' in terms of individuals and the interests of individuals. As the founders of the psychological journal *Ideology and Consciousness* have put it:

> It is not in intersubjective negotiations of meaning between persons that the social formation consists but in a structured set of material practices that are in no way reducible solely to relations between persons. (Adlam *et al*, 1977)

Marxist psychologies – where they do not reduce to Marxist politics tagged on to some more traditional psychological approach (often behaviourism or learning theory) – appear to have as their aim the reconciliation of the individual and the societal. To quote Adlam *et al* again:

> Our project is to develop an adequate theory of ideology, one sufficiently comprehensive to embrace both 'social' and 'individual' aspects. That is to say, it must be capable of addressing problems and formulating theories both in respect of social formations as a whole and in respect of the individual and his or her constitution as a subject.

In practice, however, it always seems that 'the individual', the natural focus of psychological analysis and psychologists' action, becomes displaced by concentration on 'the social'. That a line of theorizing 'ultimately reduces to a form of radical individualism' is for Adlam *et al* a very telling criticism, and this would appear to be true of much that is good in the Marxist contribution to psychological theory.

In opposition to this stance, it would seem to me at present that a competent and comprehensive critical psychology must to an extent focus on the individual.

1.   Psychology's scope is human behaviour and experience, and 'social relations' in the sociological sense enter into it only to the extent that they are experienced by the individual or impinge on his or her behaviour. This will mean, in practice, that the study of social relations will form by far the largest part of a critical psychology, because the unaware subject's experience and behaviour are largely (perhaps totally) determined by structural factors as reflected in the 'taken-for-granted' truths of the surrounding culture. To the extent that a critical psychology succeeds in its endeavours, however, people become aware

of what they had previously taken for granted. At that point the structure may still constrain, but it no longer determines.

2.   When we have discussed the relation of the individual to the broader set of social structures and social relations, we have not exhausted our potential for understanding. Social psychology has developed distinctive interests in the interactions between individuals, and how meanings and life-spaces are negotiated and mutually determined – for example in Kellian psychology, in the application of systems theory to family therapy and in the recent reimportation of the perspectives of Symbolic Interactionism – which cannot be *subsumed* under broader sociological theories. It seems strange and unnecessary to throw away these distinctively psychological insights or to treat them as of little theoretical account, when they can extend our understanding and our potential for action. (For that matter, it seems silly to throw away the insights of more strictly individual psychology or of biology and sociobiology to the extent to which these can extend our understanding.)

3.   It is of course true that the importance we give to 'the individual' and to the 'freedom' of the individual is a cultural product and potentially an enslaving one. The stress on individual interests and individual advancement is a comfortable and a convenient one for the way our society is structured – convenient because it reduces solidarity between those whose ultimate interests are *not* served by the way things are and comfortable because it provides a distracting focus of attention for those whose interests *are* served by the way things are. However, it seems to me equally true that 'the individual' and the concept of individual freedom is also one of our culture's greatest and most beneficial inventions. The aim of a critical psychology, it seems to me, should be not to suppress this cultural invention but to make it available for use. I do not believe that the inequities of current social arrangements can be changed except by people who understand what they want and what they are doing and who are alert to the human tendency to 'take things for granted'.

I have argued, therefore, that a critical psychology must take as its focus the experience and the life-space of individuals. Much of its concern will be with the ways in which we are constrained by a structure and a culture which are not designed or intended to serve our interests. Critical psychology's potential is not confined to the political level, however, important political/sociological questions may be to it. a critical psychology should have the potential to explore all aspects of human experience 'from the inside', to examine how our individual and collective worlds are shaped by factors which we generally take for granted, so that we may progressively take greater and greater control of our own 'nature'. In Shotter's words:

> . . . we have no real nature, no natural nature, because we are self-determining, self-defining animals . . . to the extent that [man] can modify or transform the quality of his own consciousness he can modify or transform himself . . . so that by understanding more clearly what we are and the situation or 'position' we occupy, we may be able to describe explicitly the possibilities available to us all for what we might do next, for what we might make of ourselves and our world.   (Shotter, 1975, pp. 11 and 14)

This book has looked briefly at the lives and experiences of a group of men who have been caught up, because of their own actions, in one of the more explicitly repressive and controlling of our social institutions in one of its most repressive and controlling aspects. It has shown, I hope, that even there life has multiple possibilities. This says nothing for the conditions of the men's imprisonment or for the society which finds it 'necessary' to impose such conditions, but much for the 'nature' of human nature.

REFERENCES

Abbot, P. and Sapsford, R. J. (1983) *Mental handicap – a peripheral problem?*, paper presented to a British Sociological Association Conference at Cardiff.

Aberbach, J. D. (1977) 'Power consciousness: a comparative analysis', *American Political Science Review*, vol 71, pp. 1544–60.

Abramovitz, S. (1969) 'Locus of control and self-reported depression among college students', *Psychological Reports, 25*, 149–50.

Abramson, L., Garber, J., Edwards, N. B. and Seligman, M. E. P. (1978b) 'Expectancy changes in depression and schizophrenia', *Journal of Abnormal Psychology, 87*, 102–9.

Abramson, L., Garber, J. and Seligman, M. E. P. (1980) 'Learned helplessness in humans: an attributional analysis', in Judy Garber and M. E. P. Seligman (eds), *Human Helplessness: Theory and Applications*, Academic Press.

Abramson, L., Seligman, M. E. P. and Teasdale, J. D. (1978a) 'Learned helplessness in humans: critique and reformulation', *Journal of Abnormal Psychology, 87*, 49–74.

Advisory Council on the Penal System (Radzinowicz Committee) (1968) *The Regime for Long-Term Prisoners in Conditions of Maximum Security*, HMSO.

Adlam, D., Henriques, J., Rose, N., Salfield, A., Venn, C. and Walkerdine, V. (1977) 'Psychology, ideology and the human subject', *Ideology and Consciousness, no 1*, 5–56.

Armistead, N. (ed) (1974) *Reconstructing Social Psychology*, Penguin.

Bailey, W. (1974) 'Murder and the death penalty', *Journal of Criminal Law and Criminology, 65*, 416–23.

Bandura, A. (1977) 'Self-efficacy: towards a unifying theory of behavioural change', *Psychological Review, 84*, 191–215.

Bannister, P. A., Heskin, K. J., Bolton, N. and Smith, F. V. (1974) 'A study of variables related to the selection of long-term prisoners for parole', *British Journal of Criminology, 14*, 359–68.

Bannister, P. A., Smith, F. V., Heskin, K. J. and Bolton, N. (1973),

'Psychological correlates of long-term imprisonment I: cognitive variables', *British Journal of Criminology*, *13*, 313–23.

Bannister, D. and Fransella, F. (1971) *Inquiring Man*, Penguin.

Barron, F. (1953) 'An ego-strength scale which predicts response to psychotherapy', *Journal of Consulting Psychology*, *17*, 327–33.

Barton, R. (1959) *Institutional Neurosis*, Bristol, Wright.

Battle, E. and Rotter, J. B. (1963) 'Children's feelings of personal control as related to social class and ethnic groups', *Journal of Personality*, *31*, 482–90.

Beck, A. T. (1967) *Depression: Causes and Treatment*, University of Pennsylvania Press.

Beck, A. T., Weissman, A., Lester, D. and Trexler, L. (1974), 'The measurement of pessimism', *Journal of Consulting and Clinical Psychology*, *42*, 861–915.

Belknap, I. (1956), *Human Problems in a State Mental Hospital*, McGraw-Hill.

Berger, P. L. and Kellner, H. (1964) 'Marriage and the construction of reality', *Diogenes*, *46*, 1–25.

Berger, P. L. and Luckman, T. (1972) *The social Construction of Reality*, Penguin.

Bettelheim, B. (1943) 'Individual and mass behaviour in extreme situations', *Journal of Abnormal and Social Psychology*, *38*, 417–52.

Bettelheim, B. (1960) *The Informed Heart*, Macmillan.

Bibring, E. (1953) 'The mechanism of depression', *in* P. Greenacre (ed), *Affective Disorders*, New York, International Universities Press.

Black, W. M. and Gregson, R. M. (1973) 'Time perspective, purpose in life, extraversion and neuroticism in a sample of New Zealand prisoners', *British Journal of Social and Clinical Psychology*, *12*, 50–60.

Bolton, N., Smith, F. V., Heskin, K. J. and Banister, P. A. (1976) 'Psychological correlates of long-term imprisonment IV: a longitudinal analysis', *British Journal of Criminology*, *16*, 38–47.

Brehm, J. W. and Sensenig, J. (1966) 'Social influence as a function of attempted and implied usurpation of choice', *Journal of Social Psychology*, *4*, 703–7.

Brehm, J. W., Skires, L. K., Sensenig, J. and Shaban, J. (1966) 'The attractiveness of an eliminated choice alternative', *Journal of Experimental Social Psychology*, *2*, 301–13.

Brickman, P., Linsenmeier, J. A. W. and McCareins, A. G. (1976) 'Performance enhancement by relevant success and irrelevant failure', *Journal of Personality and Social Psychology*, *33*, 149–60.

Broadman, K., Broadman, A. J., Lorge, I. and Wolf, H. G. (1959) 'The Cornell Medical Index: an adjunct to medical interview', *Journal of the American Medical Association*, *140*, 530.

Broadman, K., Broadman, A. J., Lorge, I., Wolf, H. G. and

Gershenson, P. (1952) 'The Cornell Medical Index – Health Questionnaire: the evaluation of emotional disturbance', *Journal of Clinical Psychology*, *119*, 119 and 550.

Calvert, E. (1927) *Capital Punishment in the Twentieth Century*, London, Putnam.

Caudill, W., Redlich, F. C., Gilmore, H. and Brody, E. B. (1952) 'Social structure and interaction processes on a psychiatric ward', *American Journal of Orthopsychiatry*, *22*, 314–34.

Chang, D. H. and Zastrow, C. H. (1976) 'Inmates' and security guards' perceptions of themselves and each other', *International Journal of Criminology and Penology*, *4*, 89–98.

Chang, D. H., Zastrow, C. H. and Blaziek, D. L. (1975) 'Inmate perception of significant others', *International Journal of Criminology and Penology*, *3*, 85–96.

Cohen, S. and Taylor, L. (1972) *Psychological Survival: the Experience of Long-Term Imprisonment*, Penguin.

Cohen, S. and Taylor, L. (1976) *Escape attempts: the theory and practice of resistance of everyday life*, Allen Lane.

Comrey, A. L. (1957a) 'A factor analysis of the MMPI hypocondriasis scale', *Educational and Psychological Measurement*, *17*, 568–72.

Comrey, A. L. (1957b), 'A factor analysis of the MMPI depression scale', *Educational and Psychological Measurement*, *17*, 573–7.

Comrey, A. L. (1958), 'A factor analysis of the MMPI psychaesthenia scale', *Educational and Psychological Measurement*, *18*, 91–8.

Council of Europe (European Committee on Crime Problems) (1977), *Treatment of Long-Term Prisoners*, Strasbourg, Council of Europe.

Crookes, T. G. (1979) 'Sociability and behaviour disturbance', *British Journal of Criminology*, *19*, 60–66.

Csikzentmihalyi, M. (1976) *Beyond Boredom and Anxiety*, Jossey-Bass.

Culpan, R. H., Davies, B. M. and Oppenheim, A. N. (1960) 'Incidence of psychiatric illness among hospital outpatients: an application of the Cornell Medical Index', *British Medical Journal*, 855.

Delavignette, R. (1950) *Freedom and authority in French West Africa*, Oxford University Press.

Dimsdale, J. E. (1974) 'The coping behaviour of Nazi concentration camp survivors', *American Journal of Psychiatry*, *120*, 241–8.

Dixon, P. (1967) *Reduced Emotional Responsiveness in Schizophrenia*, unpublished Ph.D. thesis, University of London.

Drake, L. E. (1946) 'A social IE scale for the MMPI', *Journal of Applied Psychology*, *30*, 51–4.

Drake, L. E. and Thiede, W. B. (1948) 'Further validation of the social IE scale for the MMPI', *Journal of Educational Research*, *41*, 551–6.

Dweck, C. and Repucci, N. D. (1973) 'Learned helplessness and reinforcement responsibility in children', *Journal of Personality and Social Psychology*, *25*, 109–16.

Edgell, S. (1980) *Middle-Class Couples*, Allen & Unwin.

Ellenberger, H. F. (1960) 'Zoological garden and mental hospital', *Canadian Psychiatric Association Journal*, *5*, 136–49.

Epstein S. (1967) 'Towards a unified theory of anxiety', in B. A. Maher (ed), *Progress in Experimental Personality Research*, vol 4, Academic Press.

Epstein, S. and Fenz, W. D. (1965), 'Steepness of approach and avoidance gradients in humans as a function of experience', *Journal of Experimental Psychology*, *70*, 1–12.

Eriksen, C. W. and Davids, A. (1955) 'The meaning and clinical validity of the Taylor manifest anxiety scale', *Journal of Abnormal and Social Psychology*, *50*, 135–7.

Eysenck, H. J. (1977) *Crime and Personality*, third edition, Routledge & Kegan Paul.

Farber, M. L. (1944) 'Suffering and time perspective in the prisoner', University of Iowa, *Studies in Child Welfare*, *20*, 153–227.

Fattah, E. (1972) *A survey of the deterrent effect of capital punishment with special reference to the Canadian situation*, Canada, Department of the Solicitor General, Research Centre Report no 2.

Fenz, W. D. and Epstein, S. (1967), 'Gradients of physiological arousal of experienced and novice parachutists as a function of an approaching jump', *Psychosomatic Medicine*, *29*, 33–51.

Fitch, J. H. (1962) 'The personality variables and their distribution in a criminal population: an empirical study', *British Journal of Social and Clinical Psychology*, *1*, 161–7.

Fitzgerald, M. and Sim, J. (1982) *British Prisons*, Blackwell.

Flanagan, T. J. (1981) 'Dealing with long-term confinement: adaptive strategies and perspectives among long-term prisoners', *Criminal Justice and Behaviour*, *8*, 201–22.

Fosco, E. and Geer, J. H. (1971) 'Effects of gaining control over aversive stimuli after differing amounts of no control', *Psychological Reports*, *29*, 1153–4.

Foster, T. W. (1982) "Mushfaking': a compensatory behaviour of prisoners', *Journal of Social Psychology*, *117*, 115–24.

Freud, S. (1905) 'Three essays on the theory of sexuality', in *On Sexuality*, Penguin, 1977.

Freud, S. (1917) *Introductory lectures on psychoanalysis*, Penguin, 1973.

Fromm, E. (1976) *To Have Or To Be?*, Jonathan Cape, 1978.

Gatchell, R. J., Paulus, P. B. and Maples, C. W. (1975) 'Learned helplessness and self-reported affect', *Journal of Abnormal Psychology*, *16*, 732–4.

Geer, J. H., Davison, G. C. and Gatchell, R. J. (1970) 'Reduction of stress in humans through nonveridical perceived control of aversive stimulation', *Journal of Personality and Social Psychology, 16,* 731–8.

Gibson, E. and Klein, S. J. (1969) *Murder 1957 to 1968,* HMSO, Home Office Research Study no 3.

Glaser, D. (1964) *The Effectiveness of a Prison and Parole System,* Indianapolis, Bobbs-Merrill.

Glass, D. C. and Singer, J. E. (1972) *Urban Stress: Experiments on Noise and Social Stresses,* Academic Press.

Goemann, M. (1977) *Das Schicksal der Lebenslanglichen,* Berlin, De Gruyter.

Goffman, E. (1957) 'Characteristics of total institutions', in *Symposium on Preventive and Social Psychology,* Washington, Walter Reed Army Institute of Research.

Goffman, E. (1961) *Asylums: Essays on the Social Situation of Mental Patients and Other Inmates,* New York, Doubleday.

Goss, A. and Morosko, T. E. (1970) 'Relations between a dimension of internal–external control and the MMPI with an alcoholic population', *Journal of Consulting and Clinical Psychology, 23,* 342–6.

Gottesman, I. I. (1959) 'More construct validation of the ego-strength scale', *Journal of Consulting Psychology, 23,* 342–6.

Gower Commission (1953) *Report of the Royal Commission on Capital Punishment,* London, HMSO, Cmnd 8932.

Greenson, R. R. (1949) 'The psychology of apathy', *Psychoanalytic Quarterly, 18,* 290–302.

Grinker, R. R. and Spiegel, J. P. (1945) *Men Under Stress,* Philadelphia, Blakiston.

Hall, J. A. and Taylor, S. E. (1976) 'When love is blind: maintaining idealised images of one's spouse', *Human Relations, 29,* 751–61.

Hammock, T. and Brehm, J. W. (1966) 'The attractiveness of alternatives when freedom to choose is eliminated by a social agent', *Journal of Personality, 34,* 546–54.

Haney, C., Banks, W. C. and Zimbardo, P. G. (1973) 'Interpersonal dynamics in a simulated prison', *International Journal of Criminology and Penology, 1,* 69–97.

Harlow, W. F., Suomi, S. J. and McKinney, W. T. (1970) 'Experimental production of depression in monkeys', *Mainly Monkeys, 1,* 6–12.

Hathaway, S. R. and McKinley, J. C. (1940) 'A multiphasic personality inventory (Minnesota) I: construction of the schedule', *Journal of Psychology, 10,* 249–54.

Hathaway, S. R. and McKinley, J. C. (1942) 'A multiphasic personality inventory (Minnesota) III: the measurement of symptomatic depression', *Journal of Psychology, 14,* 73–84.

Hautaluona, J. E. and Scott, W. A. (1973) 'Values and sociometric choices of incarcerated juveniles', *Journal of Social Psychology, 63,* 91.

Heather, N. (1976) *Radical Perspectives in Psychology*, Methuen.

Heskin, K. J., Bolton, N., Banister, P. A. and Smith, F. V. (1977) 'Prisoners' personality: a factor analytically derived structure', *British Journal of Social and Clinical Psychology, 16*, 203–6.

Heskin, K. J., Bolton, N., Smith, F. V. and Banister, P. A. (1974) 'Psychological correlates of long-term imprisonment III: attitudinal variables', *British Journal of Criminology, 14*, 150–57.

Heskin, K. J., Smith, F. V., Banister, P. A. and Bolton, N. (1973) 'Psychological correlates of long-term imprisonment II: personality variables', *British Journal of Criminology, 13*, 323–30.

Hiroto, D. S. (1974) 'Locus of control and learned helplessness', *Journal of Experimental Psychology, 102*, 187–93.

Hirst, P. and Woolley, P. (1982) *Social Relations and Human Attributes*, Tavistock.

Home Office (1950) *Prisons and Borstals*, HMSO.

Home Office (1974) *Report on the Work of the Prison Department, 1973*, HMSO.

Home Office (1976) *Report on the Work of the Prison Department, 1975*, HMSO.

Home Office (1980) *Report on the Work of the Prison Department, 1979*, HMSO.

Irwin, J. (1970) *The Felon*, Prentice Hall.

Jahoda, M. (1982) *Employment and Unemployment: a Social-Psychological Analysis*, Cambridge University Press.

Jahoda, M., Lazarsfield, P. E. and Zeisel, H. (1972) *Marienthal*, Tavistock Press.

Kelly, G. A. (1955) *The Psychology of Personal Constructs*, New York, Norton.

Kelly, G. A. (1969) 'Personal construct theory and the psychotherapeutic interview', *in* B. A. Maher (ed), *Clinical Psychology and Personality*, Wiley.

King, R. D. and Elliott, K. W. (1977) *Albany: Birth of a Prison – End of an Era*, Routledge & Kegan Paul.

Klein, D. C., Fencil-Morse, E. and Seligman, M. E. P. (1976) 'Learned helplessness, depression and the attribution of failure', *Journal of Personality and Social Psychology, 33*, 508–16.

Kral, V. A., Pazder, L. H. and Wigdor, B. T. (1967) 'Long-term effects of a prolonged stress experience', *Canadian Psychiatric Association Journal, 12*, 175–81.

Landau, S. F. (1969) 'The effects of length of imprisonment and subjective distance from release on future time perspective and time estimation in prisoners', Hebrew University of Jerusalem, *Scripta Hierosolymitana, 21*, 182–223.

Lawton, J. (1978) 'Some lifers' views', *Prison Service Journal*, April, 9–10.

Lefcourt, H. M. (1966) 'Belief in personal control', *Journal of Individual Psychology*, 22, 185–96.

Lefcourt, H. M. (1976) *Locus of Control: Current Trends in Theory and Research*, Wiley.

Lefcourt, H. M. and Ladwig, G. W. (1965) 'The American negro: a problem in expectancies', *Journal of Personality and Social Psychology*, 1, 377–80.

Leguin, U. (1969) *The Left Hand of Darkness*, Macdonald.

Lessing, E. E. (1968) 'Demographic, developmental and personality correlates of length of future time perspective', *Journal of Personality*, 36, 183–201.

Lichtenberg, P. A. (1957) 'A definition and analysis of depression', *Archives of Neurology and Psychiatry*, 77, 516–27.

Lubow, R. E., Caspry, T. and Schnur, P. (1982) 'Latent inhibition and learned helplessness in children: similarities and differences', *Journal of Experimental Child Psychology*, 34, 231–56.

McGinnies, E., Nordholm, L. A., Ward, C. D. and Belthumnavia, D. L. (1974) 'Sex and cultural differences in perceived locus of control among students in five countries', *Journal of Consulting and Clinical Psychology*, 42, 451–5.

McKinley, J. C. and Hathaway, S. R. (1940) 'A multiphasic person-ality inventory (Minnesota) II: a differential study of hypochondri-asis', *Journal of Psychology*, 10, 255–68.

McKinley, J. C. and Hathaway, S. R. (1942) 'A multiphasic person-ality inventory (Minnesota) IV: psychaesthenia', *Journal of Applied Psychology*, 26, 614–24.

Maier, S. F. (1970) 'Failure to escape traumatic shock: incompatible skeletal motor responses or learned helplessness?', *Learning and Motivation*, 1, 157–70.

Maier, S. F., Anderson, C. and Lieberman, D. A. (1972) 'Influence of control of shock on subsequent shock-elicited aggression', *Journal of Comparative and Physiological Psychology*, 81, 94–100.

Maier, S. G., Seligman, M. E. P. and Solomon, R. L. (1969) 'Pavlovian fear conditioning and learned helplessness', in B. A. Campbell and R. M. Church (eds), *Punishment*, New York, Appleton-Century-Crofts.

Malikiosi, M. and Ryckman, R. M. (1977) 'Differences in perceived locus of control among men and women adults and University students in America and Greece', *Journal of Social Psychology*, 103, 177–83.

Maracek, J. and Mettee, D. R. (1972) 'Avoidance of continued suc-cess as a function of self-esteem, level of esteem certainty and responsibility for success', *Journal of Personality and Social Psychology*, 22, 98–107.

Marcuse, H. (1937) 'Philosophy and critical theory', in *Negations*, Penguin, 1968.

Marcuse, H. (1955) *Eros and Civilisation*, Beacon Books.

Marcuse, H. (1958) *Soviet Marxism: a Critical Analysis*, Routledge & Kegan Paul.

Marcuse, H. (1964) *One-Dimensional Man*, Routledge & Kegan Paul.

Marcuse, H. (1969) *An Essay on Liberation*, Penguin.

Martin, D. V. (1955) 'Institutionalisation', *Lancet*, pp. 1188–90.

Marx, K. (1844) *The Eighteenth Brumaire of Louis Bonaparte*, Central Books, 1977.

Masserman, J. W. (1943) *Behaviour and Neurosis*, Chicago University Press.

Melges, F. T. and Bowlby, J. (1969) 'Types of hopelessness in psychopathological process', *Archives of General Psychiatry, 20*, 690–99.

Melges, F. T. and Weiss, A. E. (1971) 'The personal future and suicidal ideation', *Journal of Nervous and Mental Disease, 153*, 244–50.

Mettee, D. R. (1971) 'Rejection of unexpected success as a function of the negative consequences of accepting success', *Journal of Personality and Social Psychology, 17*, 332–41.

Mischel, W. and Masters, J. C. (1966) 'Effect of probability of reward attainment on responses to frustration', *Journal of Personality and Social Psychology, 6*, 390–96.

Morris, T. and Morris, P. (1961) 'The experience of imprisonment', *British Journal of Criminology, 2*, 337–60.

Morris, T. and Morris, P. (1963) *Pentonville*, Routledge & Kegan Paul.

Nardini, J. E. (1952) 'Survival factors of American prisoners of war of the Japanese', *American Journal of Psychiatry, 109*, 241–8.

Newman, P. H. (1944) 'The prisoner of war mentality', *British Medical Journal*, 8–10.

Newton, M., Hickey, P., and Huff, G. (1972) *Inmates' attitudes to imprisonment*, Home Office Prison Department, Chief Psychologist's Reports (Series D) no. 9.

Nuttall, C. P. with Barnard, E. E., Fowles, A. J., Frost, A., Hammond, W. H., Mayhew, P., Pease, K. G., Tarling, R. and Weatheritt, M. J. (1977) *Parole in England and Wales*, HMSO, Home Office Research Study no 38.

Overall, J. E. and Gomez-Mont, F. (1974) 'The MMPI-168 for psychiatric screening', *Educational and Psychological Measurement, 36*, 1111–13.

Overall, J. E., Hunter, S. and Butcher, N. (1973) 'Factor structure of the MMPI-168 in a psychiatric population', *Journal of Consulting and Clinical Psychology, 41*, 284–86.

Parker, T. (1973) (ed), *The Man Inside*, Michael Joseph.

Parole Board (1970) *Report of the Parole Board for 1969*, HMSO.

Parsons, O. A., Schneider, J. M. and Hansen, A. S. (1970) 'Internal–external locus of control and national stereotypes in Denmark and the United States', *Journal of Consulting and Clinical Psychology*, 35, 30–37.

Price, K. P. and Geer, J. H. (1972) 'Predictable and unpredictable aversive events', *Psychonomic Science*, 26, 215–16.

Quarantelli, E. I. (1954) 'The nature and conditions of panic', *American Journal of Sociology*, 60, 267–335.

Radford, R. A. (1945) 'The economic organisation of a POW camp', *Economica*, 11, 192.

Raps, C. S., Peterson, C., Reinhard, K. E., Abramson, L. and Seligman, M. E. P. (1982) 'Attributional style among depressed patients', *Journal of Abnormal Psychology*, 91, 102–8.

Rasch, W. (1977) 'Observations of physio-psychological changes in persons sentenced to life imprisonment', in Rizkalla *et al* (*op. cit.*).

Rasch, W. (1981) 'The effects of indeterminate detention: a study of men sentenced to life imprisonment', *International Journal of Law and Psychiatry*, 4, 417–31.

Reason, P. and Rowan, J. (1981) *Human Inquiry: a Sourcebook of New Paradigm Research*, Wiley.

Reitz, H. J. and Groff, G. K. (1972) 'Comparisons of locus of control categories among American, Mexican and Thai workers', in *Proceedings of the American Psychological Association*.

Richter, C. P. (1957) 'On the phenomenon of sudden death in animals and man', *Psychosomatic Medicine*, 19, 191–8.

Rizkalla, S., Levy, R. and Zauberman, R. Z. (1977) (eds), *Long-Term Imprisonment: an International Seminar*, Université de Montréal, Centre International de Criminologie Comparée.

Rogers, C. (1951) *Client-Centred Therapy*, Boston, Houghton-Mifflin.

Roth, J. A. (1963) *Timetables*, Indianapolis, Bobbs-Merrill.

Roth, S. (1980) 'A revised model of learned helplessness in humans', *Journal of Personality*, 48, 103–33.

Roth, S. and Bootzin, R. R. (1974) 'Effects of experimentally induced expectancies of external control', *Journal of Personality and Social Psychology*, 29, 253–64.

Rotter, J. B., Chance, J. and Phares, E. J. (1972) *Applications of a Social Learning Theory of Personality*, New York, Holt, Rinehart & Winston.

Saltzer, E. (1982) 'The relationship of personal efficacy beliefs to behaviour', *British Journal of Social Psychology*, 21, 213–21.

Sapsford, R. J. (1978) 'Life-sentence prisoners: psychological changes during sentence', *British Journal of Criminology*, 18, 128–45.

Sapsford, R. J. (1979a) *Learned Helplessness, Reactance and the Life-Sentence*, unpublished Ph.D. thesis, University of London.

Sapsford, R. J. (1979b) *Life-sentence prisoners: deterioration and coping*. The Open University, Social Sciences Publications.

Sapsford, R. J. and Banks, C. (1979) 'A synopsis of some Home Office research', *in* D. E. Smith 1979, *op. cit.*, 20–48.

Seligman, M. E. P. (1968) 'Chronic fear produced by unpredictable shock', *Journal of Comparative and Physiological Psychology*, 66, 402–11.

Seligman, M. E. P. (1975) *Helplessness*, San Francisco, W. H. Freeman.

Seligman, M. E. P. and Groves, D. (1970) 'Non-transient learned helplessness', *Psychonomic Science*, 19, 191–2.

Seligman, M. E. P., Maier, S. F. and Solomon, R. L. (1971) 'Unpredictable and uncontrollable aversive events', in F. R. Brush (ed), *Aversive conditioning and learning*, Academic Press.

Seligman, M. E. P. and Meyer, B. (1970) 'Chronic fear and ulcers as a function of the unpredictability of safety', *Journal of Comparative and Physiological Psychology*, 73, 202–7.

Serge, V. (1970) *Men in Prison*, Gollancz.

Shiloh, A. (1971) 'Sanctuary or prison – responses to life in a mental hospital', *in* S. E. Wallace (ed.), *Total Institutions*, New Jersey, Transaction Books.

Shotter, J. (1974) 'What is it to be human?', *in* N. Armistead (ed) *op. cit.*

Shotter, J. (1975) *Images of Man in Psychological Research*, Methuen.

Siegman, A. W. (1956) 'The effects of manifest anxiety on a concept-formation task, a non-directed learning task and on timed and untimed intelligence tests', *Journal of Consulting Psychology*, 20, 176–8.

Silverman, J., Berg, P. D. and Kantor, R. (1966) 'Some perceptual correlates of institutionalisation', *Journal of Nervous and Mental Disease*, 139, 545–9.

Sluga, W. (1977) 'Treatment of long-term prisoners considered from the medical and psychiatric point of view', in Council of Europe, *op. cit.*

Smith, D. E. (ed) (1979) *Life-sentence prisoners*, HMSO, Home Office Research Study no 51.

Smith, F. V. (1977) 'What may be attempted', *in* S. Rizkalla, R. Levy and R. Zauberman (1977) *op cit.*

Smith, F. V., Bolton, N., Banister, P. A. and Heskin, K. J. (1977) 'Investigation of the effects of long-term imprisonment', in Council of Europe (1977) *op. cit.*

Smith, R. J. (1961) 'Cultural differences in the life cycle and the concept of time', *in* R. W. Kleemeier (ed), *Aging and Leisure*, Oxford University Press.

Solzhenitsyn, A. (1968) *One Day in the Life of Ivan Denisovitch*, Penguin.

Solzhenitsyn, A. (1974) *The First Circle*, Collins.

Stanton, H. E. (1971) 'The Taylor scale – a measure of chronic anxiety or emotional reactivity?', *Australian Journal of Psychology*, 123, 69–72.

Sykes, G. (1958) *The Society of Captives*, Princeton University Press.

Taft, R. (1957) 'The validity of the Barron ego-strength scale and the Welsh anxiety index', *Journal of Consulting Psychology, 21*, 247–9.

Taylor, A. J. W. (1961) 'Social isolation and imprisonment', *Psychiatry, 24*, 373–6.

Taylor, I., Walton, P. and Young, J. (1973) *The New Criminology: for a Social Theory of Deviance*, Routledge & Kegan Paul.

Taylor, I., Walton, P. and Young, J. (eds) (1975) *Critical Criminology*, Routledge & Kegan Paul.

Taylor, J. (1953) 'A personality scale of manifest anxiety', *Journal of Abnormal and Social Psychology, 48*, 285–90.

Titmuss (1958) 'The hospital and its patients', *in* R. M. Titmuss (ed), *Essays on the Welfare State*, Allewn & Unwin.

Tittle, C. R. (1972) *Society of Subordinates*, Indiana University Press.

Toch, H. (1975) *Men in Crisis: Human Breakdowns in Prison*, Aldine.

Tokuyama, T., Tsuru, M., Hashimoto, K. and Okawa, C. (1973) 'A study on prisoners serving life sentence, third report', Japanese Ministry of Justice, *Bulletin of the Criminological Research Department*, 18–22.

Ward, D. A. and Kassebaum, G. G. (1971) 'Homosexual behaviour among women porisoners', *in* S. E. Wallace (ed), *Total Institutions*, New Jersey, Transaction Books.

Ward, J. (1973) 'Women inside', *New Society*, 16 August, 388–90.

Watson, J. B. (1930) *Behaviourism*, second edition, University of Chicago Press.

Wener, A. E. and Rehm, L. P. (1975) 'Depressive affect: a test of a behavioural hypothesis', *Journal of Abnormal Psychology, 84*, 221–7.

Wicklund, R. A. (1974) *Freedom and Reactance*, Wiley.

Williams, V. L. and Fish, M. (1974) *Convicts, Codes and Contraband*, Massachussets, Ballinger.

Wing, J. R. (1962) 'Institutionalism in mental hospitals', *British Journal of Social and Clinical Psychology, 1*, 38–51.

Wing, J. R. and Brown, G. W. (1970) *Institutionalism and schizophrenia*, Cambridge University Press.

Wortman, C. and Brehm, J. W. (1975) 'Responses to uncontrollable outcome', *in* L. Berkowitz (ed), *Advances in Experimental Social Psychology*, vol 8, Academic Press.

Zakia (1969) *Psychological Comparison of University Students With and Without Study Difficulties*, unpublished Ph.D. thesis, University of London.

Zimbardo, P. G. (1972) 'Pathology of imprisonment', *Society, 9*, 4–8.

Zimbardo, P. G. (1973) 'On the ethics of intervention in human psychological research', *Cognition, 2*, 243–56.

Author Index

Subject Index